MUSASHI

MUSASHI

William de Lange

Fact & Fiction

TABLE OF CONTENT

Introduction	vi
Musashi's Birthplace	1
Musashi's Parents	7
Musashi's Children	15
Musashi's Names	27
Musashi's Appearance	33
Musashi's Family Crest	35
Musashi's Battles	37
Musashi's Benefactors	51
Musashi's Places	63
Musashi's Duels	105
Musashi's Bouts	119
Musashi's Friends	141
Musashi's Deshi	149
Musashi's Weapons	155
Musashi's Injuries	159
Musashi's Death	161
Musashi's Burial	163
Glossary	165
Index	167

Edo
Mt. Fuji
Nagoya
Kyoto
Nara
Miyamoto
Akashi
Osaka
Himeji
Matsue
Okayama
Fukuyama
Matsuyama
Kokura
Kitsuki
Nakatsu
Kumamoto
Yatsushiro

INTRODUCTION

In the long and complicated—indeed, often hotly contended—narrative of Miyamoto Musashi's life there are a number of important questions that remain tantalizingly elusive: What was his appearance? Where was he born? Who was his father? Who was his mother? Who were his children? Who were his benefactors? In what battles did he fight? With whom did he duel? Where did he stay? And where is his grave?

Up till recently, there were not many original sources to which the English reader could turn to answer these questions about Musashi's life. Indeed, even in his *Gorin no sho* (Book of Five Rings) Musashi hardly touches on any of these questions, limiting the outlines of his life to no more than a few paragraphs before launching into his exposition on his school of swordsmanship. With the translations of the extant classic Japanese sources (published in the series: *The Real Musashi*), the English reader now has at his disposal a wholly new range of sources.

These sources nevertheless present a highly complex, at times quite bewildering array of alternative perspectives and narratives. The diligent research of many Japanese scholars, as well as amateur historians, has uncovered some two dozen extant texts in which the medieval swordsman makes his appearance, sometimes only fleetingly, at other times at great length. And while all these sources add their own piece to the checkered puzzle that is Musashi, they do so in their own idiosyncratic way, giving rise to new misunderstandings, even while they rule out old ones.

This guide seeks to bring order in that chaos by carefully reconstructing the narrative of Musashi's life. Through a clearly defined number of themes, it addresses those hitherto unanswered questions on the basis of the original Japanese sources. Unless they are waylaid by firm historical fact, it gives as much credence as possible to these early accounts, not only because they are the only true sources we have, but to do justice to the great efforts of those early historians, many of whom dedicated the better part of their lives in a serious quest to uncover all they could about the man they, like so many after them, had come to admire.

MUSASHI'S BIRTHPLACE

One of the most controversial aspects of Musashi's life is his birthplace. It is a mark of Musashi's modest origins that we do not even know with certainty the place where he was born. This is not to say that we cannot get close. Apart from Musashi's own statements, there are a great number of classic records that can help us to home in on the place in medieval Japan where japan's most famous swordsman came into the world. They can be divided into two categories: they either expound the theory that he was a native of Mimasaka, or the theory that he was a native of Harima.

The Mimasaka Narrative

The first chronicler to claim that Musashi was born in the province of Mimasaka goes to Mikami Genryū, who in his *Gekken sōdan* (1790) states that, "Master Musashi was born in the village of **Miyamoto** in the Yoshino district of Mimasaka Province." The most ardent proponent of the so-called Mimasaka-*setsu*, or the Mimasaka narrative of Musashi's origins, however, is undoubtedly Masaki Teruo. Teruo served Matsudaira Yasuchika, the *daimyō* of the Tsuyama fief in Mimasaka, as an advisor and instructor in the Kōshū-*ryū*, a school of martial arts connected to he house of Takeda Shingen.

In his *Tōsakushi* (1851), Masaki explicitly states that the *Honchō bugei shoden* (1714) is wrong in claiming that Musashi hailed from Harima. In doing so Teruo seems to go against a number of other records on Miyamoto Musashi, many of whom were written decades, if not centuries before the *Tōsakushi*. Thus the *Harima kagami* (1762) states that "Miyamoto Musashi hailed from the village of Miyamoto in the vicinity of Ikaruga in the district of Ittō." More importantly, in his *Gorin no sho*, Musashi was the first to claim that he was a native of Harima. There may, however, be specific reasons why Musashi preferred to consider himself a native of Harima, rather than Mimasaka. First of all his father, Muni, with whom he had a troubled relationship came from Mimasaka (see Musashi's Father). However, his beloved stepmother, Yoshiko, came from Harima (see Musashi's Mother). And it was near the village of Hirafuku, at the Shōrenan temple of his uncle Dōrin, that Musashi spent the happiest and most formative years of his childhood. Not surprisingly, it was in the province of Harima that Musashi settled down during the middle years of his life.

Another reason for Musashi's willing misrepresentation of his roots in his *Gorin no sho* may be that, like many of the other western provinces, the province of Mimasaka had been the breeding ground of Tokugawa dissent in the run-up to the Battle of Sekigahara (1600). Indeed, Ukita Hideie, at that time the *daimyō* of both Bizen and Mimasaka, was one of the ringleaders of the Mitsunari alliance and the first to mobilize his troops when he held a ceremony for those who would go into battle at the **Hōkoku shrine** in Fukuoka. He did so on 8 September 1600, eleven days before Ishida Mitsunari and his co-conspirators decided to move against Ieyasu at a secret conference at Mitsunari's stronghold of Sawayama castle.

Musashi wrote his *Gorin no sho* while he was the guest of Hosokawa Tadatoshi (1586–1641) whose father had been one of the first to choose Ieyasu's side in the run-up to the Battle of Sekigahara. Likewise, Musashi's former hosts, Ogasawara Tadazane (Akashi) and Nagaoka Okinaga (Kokura), both fought and earned their promotions by joining Ieyasu's side. Musashi had nothing to hide in this respect, for he had always fought among Ieyasu's allies (see Musashi's Battles), but as he had never really been in their service, he may at the same time have felt ill at ease with the idea that he was really a native of Mimasaka. Nor are some of the records that have traditionally been used by proponents of the

Harima-*setsu*, or the Harima narrative, as explicit as some historians would suggest. The *Honchō bugei shoden*, for instance, merely states that Musashi "hailed" from the province of Harima and that he was "a scion of the Shinmen, a strand of the Akamatsu." Thus one might consider someone who has been raised in Harima as someone who hails from Harima.

Equally, the *Shimoshō mura kojichō*—a record from Shimoshō village in Mimasaka Province—merely states that in 1599 Musashi "left the country for Kyushu," not specifying whether the country in question was Mimasaka or Harima. Even Musashi's son Iori seems to shy away from explicitly stating that his father was born in Harima. Thus, in the *Kokura hibun* (1654) he only mentions that Musashi was a scion of the Shinmen, the last descendants of the Akamatsu of Harima. More tellingly, in the *Tomari jinja munefuda* (1653) he states that:

作州の顕氏に神免なる者があった。天正の間、あと嗣ぎが無いまま、筑前秋月城で亡くなった。その遺を受け家を継承したのを、武蔵掾玄信という。後に宮本と改氏した。

Among the Akamatsu diaspora of the province of Mimasaka, there were those who belonged to a line called the Shinmen. During the Tenshō era, the Shinmen line came to an end at Akizuki castle in the province of Chikuzen because there was no successor. Heir to this house and heritage was a man named Musashi Genshin, who later took on the family name of Miyamoto.

Where most records are content with merely mentioning that Musashi was a scion of the Shinmen, a strand of the Akamatsu, the *Tomari jinja munefuda*—the first written record on Musashi outside those from his own hand—establishes a clear link between Musashi and the Shinmen from Mimasaka.

It is here where the *Tōsakushi* and the other records in the Mimasaka-*setsu* tradition become so compelling. They, after all, seek to shed light on Musashi's roots, his youth, and the setting in which he was raised, rather than just copying each other where it concerned his roots and just dwelling on his adventures during his later life as a swordsman.

The Harima narrative

While the widely accepted view is that Musashi was born in Miyamoto in the province of Mimasaka, especially in recent years the alternative Harima-*setsu* has won ground. The most compelling argument in its favor is Musashi's own claim that he was a native of Harima. It is supported by a number of medieval records, most prominent among them the *Honchō bugei shoden* and the *Harima kagami*.

The question, then, remains in which part of Harima he was born. Musashi. for one, was not clear on the subject, merely stating "I am a *bushi* born in Harima" (生國播磨の武士). The *Kokura hibun*, on the other hand, while it is adamant that Musashi "Died at Kumamoto in the province of Higo on 19 May in the second year of Shōhō [13 June 1645]," just says he was among the "last descendants of the Akamatsu of Harima." It does not reveal when or in what province he was born, let alone which village. The *Honchō bugei shoden* brings us little closer. All it says is that Musashi "hailed from the province of Harima and was a scion of the Shinmen, a strand of the Akamatsu."

The only record to be specific on Musashi's birthplace is the *Harima kagami*. Based on records and oral transmissions from the preceding century, it was largely compiled in 1762 by Hirano Yōsai, a physician from the village of Hirazu in Harima (today a part of the city of Kakogawa in Hyōgo prefecture). Knowledgable about the region, Yōsai claims that:

宮本武藏揖東郡鵤の邊宮本村の産也。若年より兵術を
好み、諸國を修行し、天下にかくれなく、則、武藏流
と云て、諸士に門人多し。然れとも、諸侯に仕へす。

Miyamoto Musashi hailed from the village of Miyamoto in the vicinity of Ikaruga in the district of Ittō. From an early age, he had a passion for the martial arts, traveling various countries on musha shugyō and being widely known under the heavens, for he counted many a samurai amongst his numerous acolytes by teaching his school of swordsmanship called Musashi-ryū. Yet Musashi never entered the service of any daimyō.

Ikaruga is a reference to the Ikaruga *shōen*, or Ikaruga manor, which used to belong to the great scholar-prince **Shōtoku Taishi** (not to be confused with the Ikaruga *no miya*, the prince's former palace in Nara, Yamato Province). Taishi's residence in Harima no longer exists, but the temple he founded under the same name (also known as the Hankyū temple) still stands in what is now the Taishi municipality of the Ibo district, in today's province of Hyōgo, only some ten miles east of Himeji castle.

Today, Miyamoto village no longer exists. It disappeared from the map toward the end of the nineteenth century, when the district of Itō was merged with that of Issai to create today's district of Ibo. Now it is known as the Miyamoto-*chiku*, a small residential area surrounding the Sekkai shrine, which is situated a few miles southwest of the Ikaruga temple, on the eastern bank of the Hayashida River (see Musashi's Places).

Significantly, however, Yōsai ends his description of Musashi's background with the remarkable caveat that:

此宮本武藏こと、佐用郡平＂の住・風水翁の説と相違有り。別書に之を記す。

This account of Musashi differs from that of an old man and a practitioner of the art of Feng Shui, who is a native of Hirafuku, in the district of Sayō. I [will?] write on this in a different work.

Hirafuku, of course, was the birthplace of Musashi's stepmother, Yoshiko, and the place where he spent much of his childhood at the Shōrenan temple of her brother Dōrin. Could it be that, on his extensive travels through his native province, Yōsai called at Hirafuku and met a distant descendant of Yoshiko or Dōrin? Sadly, we will probably never know, Yōsai's version of the old man's account has never been found.

MUSASHI'S PARENTS

Musashi's Father

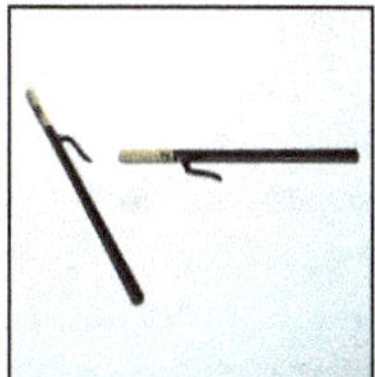

Most of the records on Musashi agree that he was the son of a scion of the Shinmen clan, who went either by the name of Muni or Munisai. Thus the *Kokura hibun*, the epitaph on the huge stone monument erected in Kokura by Musashi's son, Iori, states that the "name of his father, Shinmen, who came from a house known for its mastery of the *jitte*, was Muni." Similarly, the *Honchō bugei shoden* (1714) states that Musashi's father "was called Shinmen Munisai and was an adept in the art of the *jitte*."

The *Tōsakushi* (see Musashi's Birthplace) is the first record to claim that Muni descended from the Hirata clan. It is clear how its author, Masaki Teruo, arrived at this conclusion. Delving around in local historical records related to the Shinmen clan the historian soon found that a samurai by the name of Muni had been in the service of the Shinmen, but that his own clan's name was not Miyamoto, but Hirata. Thus a warrior by the name of Hirata Muni makes his appearance in the *Shinmen kaki*, the local record of the Shinmen clan, which Teruo already uncovered and transcribed earlier in his career:

天正六年春、草刈太郎左衛門重継猶以新免一族と数度合戦し...平田無二槍を入るゝ所に、草刈が勢引包ミ無二を打とらんと七人して鑓を付るを、平田手利にて即座に敵の鑓をからみ付、敵三人迄突留、首を取、殘る敵を追散らすにより、草刈敗軍す。

In the summer of the sixth year of the Tenshō era [1578] Kusakari Tarōemon Shigetsugu and others met in battle with the Shinmen clan several times...and when Hirata Muni advanced with his yari, seven warriors among the enemy sought to strike Muni down with their yari, but Hirata skillfully took hold of their yari, running down as many as three enemy warriors, taking their heads, and giving chase to the remainder, thereby defeating the Kusakari forces.

Muni, then, was a retainer of the Shinmen. The leader of the Shinmen clan at Muni's time was Shinmen Munetsura, the master of **Takeyama castle** in the province of Mimasaka. Early in 1554, the domains of Munetsura's father, Munesada, had been overrun by the forces of Amago Haruhisa (1514–1561), who at that time controlled no less than eight of Honshu's western provinces. Over the next few decades, his father (Munesada) had made several attempts to recover what he had lost, but all of his efforts proved abortive. Dispossessed and disillusioned Munesada passed away in 1558. The care of Munetsura, still in his infancy, was taken over by his uncle.

By the time Munetsura came of age, however, the fortunes of the Shinmen were again waxing. Their first break came with the death, in 1562, of Amago Haruhisa and then, in 1566, with the fall of their Amago stronghold of Tomida castle. Becoming enfeoffed to the powerful warlord Ukita Naoie, Munetsura gradually restored the standing of his clan in the region. During the eighties and nineties, the Shinmen held possessions in the Yoshino district totaling some five thousand *koku*, had some sixty samurai in their service, and employed close to two hundred men and women.

During these years, Munetsura served under **Ukita Hideie**, who had succeeded his father in 1582. As such Munetsura and his men had to fight in Toyotomi Hideyoshi's campaign to unify the country, as well as the two Korean campaigns during the nineties. They also had to fight at home, helping their overlord to subdue the western provinces. It is during this period, in the year 1592, that Muni again makes his appearance in the *Shinmen kaki*:

木曽判官城へ備前中納言宇喜田秀家押寄るにより、新免伊賀守勢一ツに成て戦ひ、東南の石垣を引崩す。夫より諸国勢乗込、新免方二而ハ社十右衛門、平田無二、新免備後、大原家より春名の一族、一番に乗込、首三十六取。

When Bizen Chūnagon Ukita Hideie laid siege of Hōgan castle of the Kisō clan, Shinmen Iga no Kami [Munetsura] joined forces and made battle, breeching the castle's wall on the southeast. [Hideie]'s forces now stormed in, among them Hassha Jūemon, Hirata Muni, Shinmen Higo, and all the Haruna men from the Oohara clan were the first in, taking thirty-six heads.

Muni steadily climbed in rank until, sometime during the early eighties, he reached the position of commander in charge of some fifty warriors. It was probably around this time, too, that he married Munetsura's sister (see Musashi's Mother), Omasa. For not long afterward, in 1584, she bore him his first (and only) son, whom he gave the name Bennosuke and who would on to become the one of Japan's most famous swordsman, Miyamoto Musashi.

If the *Shinmen kaki* is correct, Muni was still in the service of Shinmen Munetsura around the early 1590s. This is supported by other records, in particular the *Tōsakushi*, as well as the *Mimasaka taiheiki*, a record of the Kan clan from the Tatsuta district of Mimasaka compiled around the middle of the nineteenth century by a certain Minagi Yasuzane.

What is certain is that, by the turn of the century, Muni had moved down to Kyushu and entered the service of the Kuroda clan. That much, at least, is borne out by the *Keichō nenchū samurai-chū jija chigyō* (1604). In that document he is listed as a *furugo fudai*, or a long-standing hereditary vassal,

which, again in the code of the recordist, means that Muni had entered the service of the Kuroda before 1600, the year in which the Kuroda were promoted to their new estate in Chikuzen. Muni, in other words, had entered the service of the Kuroda before the Battle of Sekigahara. He can, therefore, not have taken part in that battle under Munetsura as many, including **Yoshikawa Eiji**, would have us believe.

In old age, probably somewhere during the first decade of the seventeenth century, Muni retired from active duty. He took the tonsure and took on the spiritual name of Munisai. He also moved again, this time to Kitsuki (see Musashi's Places), in Bungō, where he lived in a small retreat on the edge of the castle town, spending his last days in perfecting his Tōri-*ryū*. He did so on the invitation of Lord Nagaoka (Matsui) Yasuyuki (1550–1612), master of Kitsuki castle, a vassal to the powerful Hosokawa clan.

* *Yasuyuki's son, Nagaoka (Matsui) Okinaga, who had known and befriended Musashi at the time of the latter's duel with Sasaki Kojirō, would also play an important role in Musashi's old age when he took up residence in Kumamoto on the invitation of Hosokawa Tadatoshi (1586–1641). Not surprisingly, it was a retainer of the Nagaoka who, more than a century later, was to write the Bukōden, one of the first biographies of Miyamoto Musashi.*

One of the local chieftains to invite Muni for practice was the *daimyō* Kinoshita Nobutoshi, the master of Hiji castle, situated a few miles southward along the coast from the port of Kitsuki. Fortunately, Nobutoshi kept a day-to-day diary during most of 1613, and it is from this diary, the *Keichō nikki*, that it emerges that, in the spring of that year, Munisai frequently visited Hiji castle. Thus the entry for 2 May (19 June), records how, "though it had been raining since morning, Munisai came round at four o'clock." The next day, the weather improves and that evening both warriors "went out and had diner together." The dinner must have been a lavish affair, for two days later Nobutoshi was again visited by the swordsman "and was given two hats as a present."

Muni probably died during the 1620s, though the exact date is unknown. Neither has his grave ever been found. The *Tōsakushi* mentions an old tombstone among the Jigami hills, above the old family *yashiki* in Miyamoto, and assumes it must mark Muni's grave (see Musashi's Places). The grave, however, is ascribed to a certain Buni (武二), and not Muni (無二). The gravestone, then, does not mark the grave of Muni (who almost certainly died in Kyushu, probably in Kitsuki), but that of his father, *i.e.*, Musashi's grandfather. That would make the most sense chronologically, for the date on the withered stone reads "the eighteenth day of the fourth month of the eighth year of the Tenshō era [31 May 1580]."

Though the *Tōsakushi* seems to explain the source of the name Shinmen in Musashi's unabbreviated name, it is at the same time one of the most contentious aspects in the reconstruction of Musashi's life, for it means that Musashi must almost certainly have been born in the village of Miyamoto in the district of Yoshino in the province of Mimasaka and that he was therefore not a native of the province of Harima.

Musashi's Natural Mother

Musashi's Natural mother, Omasa, was the daughter of Shinmen Munesada, a minor local chieftain, who had been the lord of Takeyama castle, which was situated among the beautiful hills of the Yoshino district on the eastern border of Mimasaka Province. Early in 1554, however, Munesada's domains had been overrun by the forces of Amago Haruhisa (1514–1561). Over the next few decades, Munesada had made several attempts to recover what he had lost, but all of his efforts proved abortive. Dispossessed and disillusioned Munesada passed away in 1558.

By the time Omasa's brother, Munetsura, had come of age the fortunes of the Shinmen were again waxing. Their first break came with the death, in 1562, of **Amago Haruhisa** and then, in 1566, with the fall of their Amago stronghold of Tomida castle. Becoming enfeoffed to the powerful warlord Ukita Naoie (1529–1582), and later his son, Ukita Hideie (1572–1655), Munetsura gradually restored the standing of his clan in the region. During the eighties and nineties, the Shinmen held possessions in the Yoshino district totaling some five thousand *koku*, had some sixty samurai in their service, and employed close to two hundred men and women.

It was around this time, somewhere during the sixties, that Musashi's father, Muni, entered Munetsura's service (see Musashi's Father). A great swordsman and a specialist in the art of fighting with the *jitte*, Muni proved a valuable retainer. He gradually climbed in rank until, somewhere around the early eighties, he had reached the position of commander in charge of some fifty warriors. It was probably around this time, too, that he married Omasa, for not long afterward, in 1584, they had their first (and only) son, who received the name Bennosuke.

Sadly Omasa died in childbirth so that she would never see how her son went on to become one of Japan's most celebrated swordsmen, known by the name Miyamoto Musashi.

Musashi's Stepmother

Musashi's stepmother, Yoshiko, of whom Musashi is believed

to have been very fond, was also of noble birth. Her clan belonged to a junior line of the Akamatsu clan and Yoshiko's father, Akamatsu Shigeharu, had been the master of Rikan castle, which overlooked the town of Hirafuki, not far from Harima's border with Mimasaka. The leader of the Bessho clan when Yoshiko was still a young girl was Bessho Nagaharu (1558–80), a powerful force in the region, who commanded the respect and loyalty of many of the local chieftains. Nagaharu's headquarters were at Miki castle, some thirty miles southeast from Hirafuku, and not far from Akashi.

It was the 1570s, the time that Oda Nobunaga (1534–82) had set his mind on subduing western Honshu in his drive to unify the country. His most powerful adversaries there was the great Mori clan, whose power base lay in the western province of Aki. Nagaharu had initially supported Nobunaga's drive westward, but due to his wife's clan relations, he stubbornly refused to submit to the rule of Toyotomi Hideyoshi, at that time Nobunaga's chief general in the region.

Banding up with other local chieftains he began to attack Hideyoshi's forces, even calling in the help of the Mōri. His resistance proved so fierce that at one stage, Hideyoshi's army was forced to retreat, which so enraged the great general that he laid siege to Miki castle. Finally, in January 1580, having held out for a year and ten months, Nagaharu agreed to commit *seppuku* with his wife and children on the condition that those who had served them would be spared.

Yoshiko's father, Shigeharu, had chosen Nagaharu's side in the conflict. In 1578, shortly after Hideyoshi had laid siege of Miki castle, a force under the command of Amago Katsuhisa, the master of Kōzuki castle, situated only a few miles south of Hirafuku, laid siege of Rikan castle. The castle fell after a few weeks and Shigeharu was dispossessed. That same year, Katsuhisa's domain, in turn, was overrun by a Mōri alliance, upon which both castles fell into the hands of the Ukita, one of the Mōri's staunchest allies.

Marrying into the Shinmen had been Yoshiko's rescue from a life of hard work and constant need. Their marriage, however, failed. Following her divorce from Muni, sometime during the 1590s, Yoshiko moved back to Harima and settled down in the village of Hirafuku, the place where she had been born. She remarried, this time with a member of her own clan, a man by the name of Tasumi Masahisa. The name Tasumi (rice-field dweller), suggests that he belonged to a family of farmers, although it is believed that Masahira held the position of village elder. Unlike Rikan castle, of which only the foundations remain, the **Tasumi dwelling** has survived the centuries.

* *Though not related by blood, Musashi's second adopted son, Iori, was distantly connected to Musashi's stepmother. From the family records of the Miyamoto clan in Kokura, as well as a munafuda (a sign staked to a traditional building stating the building's donor, builder, and date of construction) recently uncovered from the Tomari Hachiman shrine of Yoneda village, it appears that Iori was born as the second son of a certain Tawara Hisamitsu, a samurai in the service of Bessho Nagaharu. Following the demise of his master, Hisamitsu took up farming near Yoneda, where he had two sons, the second of whom was Iori.*

MUSASHI'S CHILDREN

Musashi's First Adopted Son, Mikinosuke

One of the few records to make any mention of Musashi's first adopted son is the *Bushū denraiki*. It's author, Tanji Hōkin, claims Musashi met a young boy who was working as a horse handler at the Nishinomiya post station while he was traveling along the Amagasaki highroad. A lively conversation ensues between the mounted warrior and the plucky young horse handler:

武州は馬上から、じっくりとかの少年の面魂を観察して、「おい、おまえ。おれが養子にして、よい主人へ出仕させてやろう。養子になれよ」と云った。しかし、少年が申すには、「仰せはありがたいことですが、老いた親があり、このように馬子をして養っています。あなたの養子になっては、両親が困ってしまいましょう。御免ください」と断わった。

Calling down from his horse, Musashi said "hey, you! How about me adopting you and placing you in the service of a good lord?" The station boy replied "I am very grateful for your offer, but I have aging parents and am supporting them by taking care of the horses. If I were to become your adopted son my parents would surely fall on hard times, so please forgive me if I decline."

Impressed by the boy's filial piety Musashi visits the boy's parents to persuade them to let him adopt their son, who goes by the name of Mikinosuke. The record then recounts how, "On his arrival there, Musashi told the parents of his intention to adopt their son and gave them some money so that they might support themselves for the time being. He also went and visited their neighbors, asking them to look after the parents."

Though an entertaining, somewhat sentimental read, this version of events must at least be partly fictional, for we now know that Mikinosuke had already lost his natural father by the time he met his future adoptive father. That much is borne out by an ancestral record drawn up in 1696 and submitted to the administrators of the Okayama fiefdom in the province of Bizen by a certain Miyamoto Kōhei, a nephew of Mikinosuke and head of a contingent of *ashigaru* of Ikeda Masakoto (1645–1700), the master of Okayama castle, on a stipend of 250 *koku*. Kōhei was fifty-five at the time, which means that, though he never knew Mikinosuke, he might have known Musashi's other adopted son, Iori, who must have visited the neighboring province of Harima regularly during the reconstruction of the Tomari shrine (see below).

Titled the *Hōkōsho*, Kōhei's ancestral record claims that Mikinosuke was in fact the third son of Nakagawa Shimanosuke, a descendant of the lord of Nakagawabara castle in the province of Ise. Next to nothing is known about Lord Shimanosuke, except that, having served **Sengoku Hidehisa** (1552–1614) for a while in his early youth, he entered the service of Mizuno Katsunari, a close vassal of Tokugawa Ieyasu, and the man under whom Musashi served in the siege of Osaka castle (see Musashi's Battles). Like Musashi, Shimanosuke joined Katsunari in battle during the siege. He did so as a *musha bugyō*, or Magistrate of Warriors, and it is almost certain that he lost his life in the siege, for he disappears from the records in the wake of the battle.

Bearing this in mind, not all of the above account may be fictional. The Nishinomiya post station, after all, is only a few miles west from Osaka, the place that saw such heavy fighting during the winter and summer sieges of Osaka castle. Having lost his father in the summer siege of the castle, Mikinosuke might indeed have ended up working as a horse-handler in Nishinomiya. It is more likely, however, that Musashi had already met and befriended Mikinosuke's father before he fell in battle and took it upon him to look after his underaged son. Indeed, it might well have been Shimanosuke's dying wish that he do so.

Following the battle, Musashi seems to have taken the boy to Hirafuku, where his beloved stepmother, Yoshiko, was still living with her new husband, Tasumi Masahisa (see Musashi's Mother). What is certain is that, sometime after 1617, Mikinosuke entered the service of **Honda Tadatoki** (1596–1626). Tadatoki was the second son of Honda Tadamasa (1575–1631), whom Musashi had probably befriended during the siege. 1617 had been the year in which Tadamasa was promoted to the prestigious domain of Himeji. As the new master of Himeji castle, he had put his son in control of the Nitta-*han*, another fiefdom in Harima of some ten thousand *koku* in size, although it had no castle and Tadatoki probably resided at Himeji castle.

In the spring of 1626, however, disaster struck when, wholly unexpectedly, Lord Tadatoki was taken ill with tuberculosis. By the middle of May Tadatoki's health had deteriorated so much that he was unable to walk and forced to keep to his quarters in Himeji castle. For several more weeks he clung on to life, nursed by his devoted wife, the beautiful Senhime (who was the daughter of Tokugawa Hidetada), and his two pages, Mikinosuke and Iwahara Gyūnosuke. Tadatoki passed away on the last day of July. His remains were buried on the temple grounds of the **Engyō temple** in Himeji. They were interred with those of his only son, who had died in infancy only five years earlier.

Tadatoki was only thirty when he passed away, but in a society that put such store in the loyalty to one's lord and master Musashi knew the fate that now lay in store for Miki-nosuke. The *Bushū denraiki* describes how:

武蔵は、そのころ大坂に居て、この事を聞き、「近日中に造酒之助が来るだろう。生涯の別れに、ご馳走してやろう」とのことである。かくて、しばらくして造酒之助がやって来た。武州は悦びに堪えず、盛大に饗応なさった。造酒之助は盃を所望して頂戴し、「これからすぐに姫路へ行くつもりです」と申し伝えた。「もっともの覚悟である」との武州の挨拶の言葉があった。造酒之助は姫路に至り、追腹したという。

Hearing of his lordship's death, Musashi, who was then at Osaka, thought "Mikinosuke will presently come and visit me. We will have to part in this life. I'll treat him to a feast." And surely, after some time, Mikinosuke came. Musashi was beside himself with joy and treated his adopted son to a banquet on a grand scale. Then, having toasted with his adoptive father, Mikinosuke said "after this, I immediately intend to make my way to Himeji cas-tle." Musashi saluted him with the words "it is becoming in you that you are thus prepared." It is said that Mikinosuke then went to Himeji castle, where he followed his lord in death.

It was considered common practice in Mikinosuke's time to immolate oneself on the death of one's lord, a practice called *junshi*. As tradition required, he did so in front of his master's grave on the sixth day following the latter's demise. He was only twenty-three years old. Had his lord passed away half a century later, Mikinosuke would have been barred from following him in death, for in 1663 the Edo Bakufu prohibited the practice by military decree.

Miyamoto Mikinosuke's grave can still be visited on the temple grounds of the Engyō temple. His grave is situated behind that of Honda Tadatoki and its inscription reads "Miyamoto Mikinosuke, Adopted son of Miyamoto Musashi: Having served Tadatoki and committed *seppuku* in front of his master's grave, a native of Ise, and adopted son of Musashi, aged twenty-three." Immediately behind Mikinosuke's grave is that of Mikinosuke's retainer, Miyata Kanbei. As Mikinosuke's retainer, it was Kanbei's role—and distinct privilege—to serve as his *kaishaku*, the person whose role it was to behead the one committing *seppuku* and thus relieve him from the terrible pain that accompanied this ritual. Left to Mikinosuke's grave is that of Tadatoki's only other page, Iwahara Gyūnosuke.

Musashi's Second Adopted Son, Iori

There are two important records that can be traced to Musashi's second adopted son, Iori: the *Kokura hibun*, and the *Tomari jinja munefuda*. The former was written on Iori's request by Akiyama Wanao (1618–73), abbot of the Taishō temple in Kumamoto (see Musashi's Friends). The latter was written following the reconstruction of the Tomari shrine.

Situated near the village of Yoneda (now a township of Kakogawa city), the **Tomari shrine** was the family shrine of the Tawara clan. In Iori's time, the shrine had fallen into disrepair, and it was somewhere during the early fifties that Iori and a number of locals undertook to restore the shrine. Work was completed in May 1653. To commemorate the occasion two *munefudas* (narrow strip of thin wood stating the construction's donors, builder, and date of completion) were attached to the inner beams of the shrine's upper structure. The *Tomari jinja munefuda* (1653) explain why Iori was so keen to preserve the shrine:

私の祖先は、六十二代・村上天皇の第七王子、具平親王より流伝して、赤松氏の出である。高祖刑部大夫持貞の代になると、時運がふるわなかった。故に、その

顕氏を避けて、田原に改称し、播州印南郡河南庄米
堕邑に住み、子孫代々ここに産まれた。

My ancestors are from the house of Akamatsu, descendants from Tomohira Shinnō, the seventh son of the sixty-second emperor Murakami. At the time of our distant ancestor Akamatsu Mochisada, an official at the Ministry of Justice, the clan fell on hard times. Being forced to shun the name of Akamatsu, they took on the name of Tawara and settled in the village of Yoneda, in the Kanan manor, in the district of Inami, in the province of Harima, where their children and their children's children were born.

Iori, then, was a scion of the Tawara of Harima. Family records of the Tawara clan furthermore reveal that he was born on 13 November 1612 as the second son of a certain Tawara Hisamitsu, a samurai in the service of **Bessho Nagaharu** (1558–80), the lord of Miki castle (also see Musashi's Mother). In 1578 Toyotomi Hideyoshi had laid siege to Miki castle, and having held out for a year and ten months, in January 1580, Nagaharu and his family agreed to commit *seppuku* on the condition that those who had served them would be spared. Reduced to the life of a *rōnin*, Tawara Hisamitsu took up farming near Yoneda, where he had two children, the second of whom was Iori.

According to the *Bukōden*, Hisamitsu had just passed away at the time Musashi met Iori. Hisamitsu had two children, a son and a daughter, but the latter had been married off to a man from the village. The boy's mother had passed away earlier, so that the boy was living alone in a small hut, surviving on the little produce yielded by a wild plot of land in the shadow of the mountains. Though probably somewhat fictionalized, the *Bukōden* describes how, when passing through Iori's hometown on one of his *musha shugyō*, Musashi first spotted the boy catching loaches in a wet paddy field beside the road along which Musashi was traveling and that it was not much later that Musashi decided to adopt Iori.

Apart from mentioning that Musashi took pity on the boy, the *Bukōden* does not dwell on Musashi's motives in adopting Iori—nor do any of the other extant records, for that matter. One of the reasons Musashi decided to do so, however, may well have been that, though not related, Iori was distantly connected to Musashi's stepmother, Yoshiko. She, after all, was the daughter of Bessho Shigeharu, master of **Rikan castle**, and a close relative of Hisamitsu's demised lord, Bessho Nagaharu (see Musashi's Mother). The *Bukōden*'s version of events is largely confirmed by the *Harima kagami*, a topography of Harima Province compiled in 1762 by Hirano Yōsai. Like the *Bukōden* it states that Iori's father "was formerly a samurai at Miki castle of the Bessho clan, but following the fall of the castle, he moved to the village of Yoneda, where he sired Iori."

The one true discrepancy between the two documents seems to be the place where Musashi met Iori: the *Bukōden* claims it was near the village of Shōhōji in the northern province of Dewa (today's Akita prefecture, while the *Harima kagami*—in accordance with Iori's own writings—claims it was Yoneda. Masanaga's claim, then, seems farfetched, but this is not necessarily the case. Old maps reveal that there used to be a village by the name of Shōhōji at that time, and that village was situated in the province of Harima. Significantly, no village by that name has ever been discovered on old maps of Dewa. The village in Harima has long since disappeared from Japanese maps, which is probably the reason why (in more recent times) it was assumed there must once have been a village by that name in Dewa. Shōhōji was situated some ten miles north of Akashi castle, in the Miki district of Harima Province. In fact, it is still called Shōhōji, today, although it is now part of the Bessho township of Miki city.

Having adopted a second son, Musashi now felt responsible to secure the boy a safe future. Musashi, at this time, was residing at the nearby castle town of Akashi on the invitation of **Ogasawara Tadazane** (1596–1667), having been asked by the latter to design Akashi's new castle gardens. (Aware that the boy did not have warrior's blood running through his veins, he decided to secure the boy a different vocation. The *Bushū denraiki* mentions how, in the course of a conversation with Lord Tadazane, Musashi said: "by the way, I have a child in my care…He is no good for sword fighting, but he could serve you and may be of use when carrying errands to the council of elders and the like."

Tadazane accepted Musashi's offer and took Iori into his service. This was in 1628. When, in 1632, Tadazane's was promoted to the Kokura fief in Kyushu, Iori moved down with him. It seems that Iori turned out to be a talented man, prudent, and endowed with a good sense of judgment. Having served a succession of Ogasawara notables, he eventually rose to the rank of chief retainer, with a fief of five thousand *koku*. According to the *Bushū denraiki* he enjoyed such standing among his peers that even:

天下のご老中も、伊織をよくご存知になられ、世上でも名臣と噂するほどの者である。譜代の家臣たちは、敷居を隔てて坐し、道路を行くにも、伊織に塵がかかってはいけないと、二間ほど先を行かせ、残る面々は一列に後から行った。そんな具合でも、少しも、不遜とも奢るとも見えなかったそうな。

The elders of the realm [the Bakufu] were well acquainted with Iori, so much so that he was highly esteemed, even among the commoners. The various generations of Ogasawara retainers would not be allowed to sit in the same room with him and when they accompanied him on the road they would keep a reverend distance of several yards for fear of soiling his attire with their splashing, thus forming a long row behind him. Yet in spite of this, he did not display the slightest disrespect or pride.

Following the move to Kokura, according to the *Harima kagami*, Iori also "went out on the battlefield during the Shimabara rebellion, during which he rendered distinguished and meritorious service, and in reward for which his fief was increased in size to three thousand *koku*." It seems that, though he may not have made a good swordsman, Iori was not wholly without military skills. Iori passed away on 18 May 1678 at the age of sixty-six.

Iori's remains were originally buried beside the monument he had erected for his father in 1654, nine years after Musashi had passed away. The monument stands on the crest of Temukeyama, a small hill, some two hundred feet in height looking out over the island of Funashima on which Musashi once dueled with Sasaki Kojirō. Temukeyama lies on the outskirts of Akazaka, situated in the northern district of the port of Kokura, which at the time lay within Iori's fief in the district of Kikunokōri.

In 1887, the area underwent reconstruction to accommodate a gun battery guarding the Strait of Shimonoseki over which it looks. (The previous year the country had been shaken by the Nagasaki Incident, and tension between Japan and China was rising, a tension that was to result in the first Sino-Japanese War seven years later). The monument was transferred to the nearby Enmeiji-yama (Akazaka), while **Iori's grave** was transferred to the southern foot of Temukeyama. Since then, Musashi's monument has been returned to its rightful place, at the top of Temukeyama, but the graves of Iori and his descendants still remain at the foot of the hill, close to the entrance of what is now called Temukeyama park.

Musashi's "Third" Adopted Son, Kurōtarō

If we are to believe the *Hōkōsho* (see above) Mikinosuke had a younger brother by the name of Kurōtarō. This Kurō-tarō would go on to have two sons, the second of whom was Kōhei, the author of the *Hōkōsho*. This record, which is still held among the archives of the University of Okayama, claims Kurōtarō was living with Mikinosuke when the latter was in the service of Honda Tadatoki (1569–1626). This would suggest that Musashi might not only have adopted Mikinosuke after the siege of Osaka castle, but also his younger brother, Kurōtarō.

The *Tōsakushi* is the only other record to suggest Musashi might have had another son. Confusingly, it claims that the boy was called Shume and that he "was in the service of the Lord of **Kokura castle**, from the house of Ogasawara, and became a chief retainer with a fief of three thousand *koku*." Obviously, its author, Masaki Teruo, who served Matsudaira Yasuchika, the *daimyō* of the Tsuyama fief in Mimasaka, is confusing things. It was, of course, Iori, who served Ogasawara Tadazane and moved to with him to Kyushu when the latter was promoted to the Kokura fief.

No other record makes any mention of Kurōtarō (or a boy called Shume, for that matter) in connection to Musashi. It is quite possible, therefore, that Mikinosuke took his younger brother under his care on his own account, after he had entered Honda Tadatoki's service sometime after 1617 (the year in which Tadatoki was promoted to his new fief of Nitta in Harima).

Kurōtarō, according to the *Hōkōsho*, succeeded his brother after the latter had followed his master in death in 1626 at the age of twenty-three. Kōhei claims that, following Tada-toki's death, Kurōtarō accompanied his widow, Senhime, and their daughter, Katsuhime, on a visit to Edo with their stepfather Honda Tadamasa under the *sankin kōtai* system. Katsuhime later married Ikeda Mitsumasa (1609–82), which is how Kōhei came to enter the service of the Ikeda clan. As pointed out above, Kōhei became the head of a contingent of *ashigaru* of Mitsumasa's son, Ikeda Masakoto (1645–1700) on a stipend of two-hundred-and-fifty *koku*.

Interestingly, while Kurōtarō is often referred to as Musashi's third adopted son, technically, he would have been Musashi's second adopted son, making Iori Musashi's third adopted son. Kurōtarō, after all, had been orphaned along with his brother in 1615, when their father fell in the summer siege of Osaka castle. If Musashi indeed also took Kurōtarō under his wings along with Mikinosuke following the siege, he would have done so several years before he adopted Iori.

Musashi's Natural Daughter

According to the *Bushū denraiki* Musashi had an affair in old age with a woman. She bore him a child—a baby girl. It describes he was besotted with the child, but that at the age of three it suddenly fell ill and died:

武州は、悲嘆限りなく、朝から夕方まで小児の死骸を膝に置いて、嘆き暮らされた。さまざまに申し上げ慰めても、一向に聞き受けられない。武州には不似合な行いだと、随仕の面々もいう...その後、死骸を葬ったのかとも問われなかった。生涯、その女児の話をされることはなかったという。

Musashi was inconsolable with grief and wept from dawn till dusk while he cradled the remains of the infant in his lap. People tried to console him but he did not hear them. Even his followers said that this was unbecoming in their master...I did not even hear whether he buried the remains, for throughout his life Musashi never again talked about the baby girl.

Remarkably, it's author, Tanji Hōkin, is one of the few to make any mention of Musashi's relation with women and the only one to mention the birth of a child. There are, however, good reasons why Hōkin should be the only one to mention this tragic episode. One reason is that the child was born out of wedlock. Not surprisingly, as suggested by Hōkin himself, Musashi never again mentioned the deeply painful event to anyone.

Another reason might be found in the kind of liaison that produced the child. Hōkin describes the woman as an *omoimono*, a word that can mean either a loved one or a prostitute, but there are strong reasons to suspect that the woman who was the object of Musashi's affections belonged to the latter. And while it was quite normal in Musashi's day for men to frequent the Yoshiwara pleasure quarters of Edo and the like, any child that was the product of such relationships was an embarrassment. It is only to Musashi's credit, then, that he deeply loved the child. Yet it is also understandable that, if Musashi's other early biographers were even aware of the liaison and its product, they balked at committing it to paper. All of them, after all, were his disciples by descent and their chief aim was to extoll the virtues of their master, rather than expose his failings, however human.

It is not surprising, then, that the only other source to make mention of such a liaison is Shoji Kasutomi, the sixth generation descendant of Shoji Jineimon, the founder of the Yoshiwara pleasure quarters in Edo. In his *Dōbō goen*, he writes that "among the women of the establishment of Kawai Kenzaemon in Shinmachi there was a courtesan by the name of Kumoi who had a liaison with Miyamoto Musashi." Writing his work in 1720, seven years before Hōkin was to complete his own, Jineimon cannot have had any knowledge of the *Bushū denraiki*, nor is it, given the geographical divide, likely that Hōkin had read the *Dōbō goen*.

MUSASHI'S NAMES

Names are one of the most inconstant factors in medieval Japanese texts. Birth, coming of age, succession, profession, high office, retirement, and death all had to find their expression in a person's name. Indeed, there are few, if any, persons of any significance in medieval Japan who went through life under one single name. Musashi himself is a case in point. In all, there are some nine different names ascribed to Musashi, all associated with a different period in his life, arising from different contexts in which he was mentioned, or used as a way to express reverence by individuals who occupied a different status in life than Musashi.

According to the *Bushū denraiki,* Musashi's infant name, or *yōmyō* (幼名), was Bennosuke (弁助). This would have been the name by which he was known until he reached the age of his so-called *genpuku,* the Shinto ceremony marking a boy's entry into adult life, usually before the age of twenty. For this Bennosuke and his father would have visited the shrine of their family patron, where Muni would have presented Bennosuke with his adult attire, have his forehead shaven (see Musashi's Appearance), and given him his adult name of Harunobu (玄信). This was probably sometime during the period he and his father had reconciled and both were living in the port of Nakatsu, on the northern shore of the island of Kyushu.

It is not certain where Muni derived the name of Harunobu, yet everything suggests that he was alluding to the great warlord Takeda Shingen (1521–73), whose given name was also Harunobu, though spelled somewhat differently (晴信). This part of Musashi's given name is perhaps least understood, as it is often read as Genshin. The cause for this confusion is the fact that, in old age, Muashi took on the Dharma name of Genshin, which is written with the exact same characters as

Harunobu, but pronounced according to the *on-yomi*, or the Chinese-style reading of the characters. This way of reading a given name, called *yūsoku-yomi* (有職読み), was particularly prominent among scholars and literati. According to Japanese tradition, during most of one's lifetime one's given name, *imina* (諱) or *mana* (真名), is pronounced according to the *kun-yomi*, which is the Japanese reading of the Chinese character, hence Harunobu. In his younger years, then, his given name would have been pronounced as Harunobu and not Genshin.

In the face of pending death, Musashi had to address another important aspect of his life as a warrior: how to assess his life's accomplishments and find peace with his own mortality. He did so in time-honored fashion: by taking on a so-called Dharma name, or *dōgo* (道号). These spiritual names were bestowed on warriors when they took the tonsure and pronounced by their *on-yomi*. Both the *Bushū denraiki* and the *Bukōden* mention that, during Musashi's last years in Kumamoto, his monastic friend Akiyama Wanao (1618–73) gave him the spiritual name of Niten Dōraku (二天道楽), which may be crudely translated as the "Niten dilettante." Niten, of course, was a reference to his renamed school of swordsmanship, the Niten Ichi-*ryū*.

The same is true for posthumous names, although these were referred to as *oku-rina* (諡). Thus the *Tōsakushi* claims Musashi's posthumous name was Genshin Niten (玄信二天). Interestingly, Musashi's given name of Harunobu, as well as his posthumous name of Genshin, is spelled with the exact same characters as the Dharma name of **Takeda Shingen** (信玄), although in reverse order—another strong indication that Muni was alluding to the great warlord when he named his son.

In medieval Japan, however, it was considered a grave insult to address someone by their given name, especially by someone lower in status. It was believed that to pronounce some-one's given name gave the speaker leverage over their spirit, reasons for which it would sometimes be invoked when putting a spell on someone. Real names, therefore, were only used by those who were senior in position to their bearers, such as one's father or one's lord. People of the same status were expected to address a person by his so-called *kemyō* (仮名) or *tsūshō* (通称), being a person's com-mon name. In Harunobu's case, this was Musashi (武蔵).

It is not certain from where Muni took the name of Musashi. Yet it is quite likely that Muni was inspired by the beautiful plains of Musashi, through which he would undoubtedly have traveled on his many visits to Edo. Situated west of Edo the plains stretched all the way from Yotsuya to the Pacific coast. Already in 1290 the court lady Gofukakusa Nijō (1258–1306) recorded in her diary how struck she was by the beauty of the plains, as she returned from a pilgrimage to the Zenkō tem-ple in Nagano in the autumn. Its vast, undulating fields of pampas grasses, she recorded, "grow so tall that even a man on horseback disappears from view." After three days of trav-eling she had lost all sense of where she was.

For his many *deshi*, as well as his later followers, it would have been unthinkable to address the swordmaster either by the name Musashi or Harunobu. Instead, they would use a so-called sobriquet or *sonshō* (尊称) to express their reverence for their master. Thus, Tanji Hōkin generally refers to him as Bushū (武州), the old way of referring to the province of Musashi, by way of expressing his respect. Hence the book's title *Bushū denraiki*, or "An Introduction to Bushū." The same is true for the *Bukōden*, although its author instead uses the honorary title of Bukō (武公), or military leader.

As was quite common in Japan and elsewhere at the time, it was from his birthplace of Miyamoto (宮本), either in Harima of Mimasaka, that Musashi derived his common family name, or *myōji* (名字). Hence, by the time the swordsman has reached the age of twenty-one, and he fights his series of duels with the members of the Yoshioka clan, he is referred to by most of the records as Miyamoto Musashi. The *Yoshioka-den*, simply refers to Miyamoto Musashi, although it claims that Musashi hailed from the northern province of Echizen. The same is true for the *Harima kagami*, which clearly links the swordsman's name to the eponymous village in Harima. The *Tōsakushi* also refers to him as Miyamoto Musashi, though it claims he was a native of Mimasaka (see Musashi's Birthplace).

Many of the early records refer to the swordsman not by the name of Miyamoto, but by his father's family name of Shinmen (新免). Thus, at the outset of his biography, Hōkin introduces his subject as Shinmen Musashi no Kami Genshin (新免武蔵守玄信), Similarly, the *Bukōden* introduces him as "master Shinmen Musashi Fujiwara Genshin." It seems that the early biographers simply followed the example of Musashi's son, Iori, whose monument to his father reads "Epitaph of Shinmen Musashi Genshin."

The *Honchō bugei shoden* introduces another variant, namely Miyamoto Musashi Seimei (宮本武蔵政名). It is not clear from where its author, Hinatsu Shigetaka, derived the name Seimei. In all likelihood, it had its origin in one of Musashi's early schools of swordsmanship, which, according to the same record, was called Hinoshita Kaizan Shinmei Miyamoto Musashi Seimei-*ryū* (日下開山神明宮本武蔵政名流). The more widely known name of Musashi's style of swordsmanship, however, was Enmei-*ryū*. The only other records to refer to Musashi by the name of Seimei are the *Tōsakushi* and the *Mimasaka ryakushi*, yet it is quite certain that both records simply followed Shigetaka's example.

Yet another variation on the same name is presented by the *Heidō kagami* one of the first records attributed to Musashi. A short treatise of a few dozen articles on his art of swordsmanship, it is signed Miyamoto Musashi no Kami

Fujiwara Yoshitsugu (宮本武蔵守藤原義輕). Today, several copies of the *Heidō kagami* exist, though their provenance is disputed by Japanese historians. It was very common in Musashi's day to use pen names, or *gō* (號), but Yoshitsugu would not have been a logical choice. Niten, however, would have been, and Musashi did indeed use that name in some of his letters (even before he moved to Kumamoto).

The final word on Musashi's real name should, of course, be given to the swordsman himself. In his *Book of Five Rings* Musashi introduces himself as Shinmen Musashi no Kami Fujiwara Harunobu (新免武蔵守藤原玄信). It is clear why Musashi did so. Shinmen, after all, was the clan into which his father had married. They were also an ancient breed of warriors who had been involved in **Emperor Go-Daigo's** (1288–1339) attempt to restore powers to the throne. That involvement had led to exile, an exile from which they were eventually allowed to return and resume their role under the name of Shinmen, or "newly absolved." Given that his father was a Shinmen, for Musashi, his family name (名字), or *kamei* (家名) was also Shinmen.

Less easy to explain is Musashi's claim to Fujiwara descent. The Fujiwara had ruled the realm by proxy throughout the Heian period (794–1185). As such they had successfully kept in check two great military clans, the Taira and the Minamoto, thereby maintaining the effeminate world of the court nobility. That world had been swept away by the ascent of the Taira (Heike), the great military clan from the province of Ise, who finally lost out to the Minamoto (Genji) in the epic Genpei War (1180–85). From then onwards, court rule had made way for a world of martial rule that would last for more than six centuries.

* *Musashi's way of presenting his name (whether it is in the* Heidō kagami, *or his* Book of Five Rings) *is the traditional*

way of presenting all one's various names—indeed, he was probably the only one with the freedom to do so. This required that one's names should be presented in the order: kamei, kemyō, uji, and imina. Thus, his family name was Shinmen, his common name was Musashi, his ancestral name was Fujiwara, and his given name was Harunobu.

MUSASHI'S APPEARANCE

The most widely known image of Musashi that has come down to us is that of a warrior somewhat advanced in years, wearing long white robes and a red *haori* and holding his iconic long and short swords in a somewhat passive stance, as if patiently awaiting his opponent's opening attack, or maybe even just for the purpose of posing for his painting. Executed in color on paper in a detailed, realistic style, it is now kept in the Shimada Museum of Art in Kumamoto.

Though the painting is attributed to Musashi himself, it might also have been painted at a later date. In that case, its painter might have based his depiction on what he had read in Tanji Hōkin's *Bushū denraiki*, one of the few documents to describe at length Musashi's physical appearance and clothing habits:

繻子の小袖に紅裏をして、足の甲に垂る程長きを着し、繻子純子又は紙子等の胴肩衣を着し、刀脇指は木柄にて、赤金拵なり。

He used to wear a long satin undergarment lined with red silk that would reach down to the arches of his feet. On top of this, he would wear a sleeveless jacket made of satin, damask, or just hemp. The hilts of his sword and daggers were made of wood decorated with copper.

However, it is just as likely that Hōkin had seen the painting whilst visiting Kumamoto and based his description on Musashi's self-portrait.

Sadly, there are no contemporary images of Musashi as a young man, let alone in his youth, though it is safe to assume that the hair on his forehead would have been shaven at the time he underwent his so-called *genpuku*, the Shinto ceremony marking a boy's entry into adult life, usually before the age of twenty (see Musashi's Names). However, it seems that later in life he took up the habit of letting his hair grow ong —so much so that, according to the *Bushū denraiki*, "his hair would grow down to his belt, although when he grew old it merely reached his shoulders."

The *Watanabe kōan taiki-wa*, the biography of the swordsman-adventurer Watanabe Kōan, who might have met Musashi in 1637 during the suppression of the Shimabara Rebellion (see Musashi's Battles), is one of the few other records to mention Musashi's physical habits, especially where it concerned his hygiene:

洗足行水を嫌いて一生沐浴する事なし。外へ跣にて
出、よごれ候えば是を拭せ置く也。それゆえ衣服よ
ごれ申す故、色目を隠すためにびろうど両面の衣服
を着る。

Musashi hated to wash his feet or clean himself with water, and never once throughout his life took a bath. Going out on bare feet he would merely wipe them, even if they were soiled. Moreover, since his clothes were dirty, he would wear a velvet coat to disguise the stains.

In a culture obsessed with physical cleanliness Musashi's habit of washing himself with no more than a wet cloth becomes less of an enigma when we realize that from an early age he had suffered from eczema. Eczema is exacerbated by dryness of the skin and those who suffer from this affliction often find relief in keeping their skin moist. This still does not seem to explain why Musashi should have shied away from taking baths, but baths in Japan are traditionally taken very hot, which, though providing some instant relief, tends to dissolve the natural oils contained in one's skin, thus resulting in an even dryer skin.

MUSASHI'S FAMILY CREST

Light on Musashi's family crest is shed by the *Hōkōsho*, an ancestral record drawn up in 1696, and submitted to the administrators of the Okayama fiefdom in the province of Bizen by a certain Miyamoto Kōhei. Kōhei was a nephew of Mikinosuke and the head of a contingent of *ashigaru* of Ikeda Masakoto (1645–1700), the master of Okayama castle, on a stipend of 250 *koku*. Kōhei was fifty-five at the time he drew up the *Hōkōsho*, which means that, though he never knew Mikinosuke, he might have known Musashi's other adopted son, Iori, who must have visited the neighboring province of Harima regularly during the reconstruction of the Tomari shrine (see below).

Also titled the Miyamoto *Kōhei senzo-zuke*, or the ancestral records of Miyamoto Kōhei, the *Hōkōsho* states that:

養祖父宮本三木之助儀、中川父志摩之助世倅にて御
座候、私ためには實の伯父にて御座候。宮本武蔵と
申す者の養子に仕り、児小姓の時分　本多中務様へ
罷出、知行七百石下され、御近衆に召仕われ候、九
曜巴紋に付け候へと仰せをもって、唯今に付け来り
申し候、御替御紋と承り候、　圓泰院様、寬永三年
寅五月七日　御卒去の刻、同十三日、二十三歳にて
御供仕り候、

Now my so-called adoptive grandfather [sic], Miyamoto Mikinosuke, was Nakagawa Shimanosuke's son, and thus in reality my uncle. He was the adopted child of a man who called himself Miyamoto Musashi and entered the service of master Honda Tadatoki as a page when still young on a stipend of 700 koku. As one of his servants, he was allowed to wear the crest of the Nine Whirlwinds, which was his lordship's alternative family crest.

The origin of the *tomo-e* as a design in family crests is uncertain. The comma-like shape is believed by some to originate in the leather guard worn by archers on their left wrist to

protect them from the impact of the bowstring after it had been released. The guard was called a *tomo*, hence the name *tomo*-e, or "picture of the *tomo*." Others trace the pattern to mainland China, where such patterns can be found on ancient artifacts. In Japan, comma-shaped jewels have been found in prehistoric tomb sites, although their symbolic meaning is unclear.

The ***tomo-e*** was first introduced as a heraldic pattern during the tenth or eleventh century and quickly caught on through its bold yet graceful simplicity. It was so popular that by the late Heian period (794–1185), it had become a ubiquitous design, not only in heraldry but also under the eaves and on the edges of the roof tiles of temples. The latter application had much to do with the belief that the *tomo*-e represented a whirlpool and could thus protect the building from water damage. Through its association with temples the *tomo*-e gradually acquired a religious connotation, so that by Musashi's time, it had become the symbol of Hachiman (八幡), the god of war.

MUSASHI'S BATTLES

The Battle of Ishigakihara

Perhaps one of the most stubborn (and at the same time most difficult to rectify) ideas is that, in 1600, Musashi should have fought among the western forces in the great battle of unification at Sekigahara. This is all the more curious since not a single one of the many sources that are available claims that Musashi (who was only sixteen years of age at the time) should have done so. Indeed, the *Bushū denraiki*, which does dwell at length on Musashi's whereabouts at this time, unequivocally states that, while the battle of Sekigahara was raging at the heart of the main island of Honshu, the young Musashi was far away on the southern island of Kyushu, taking part in the siege of Tomiku castle on behalf of his father's lord, Kuroda Yoshitaka:

出陣して、冨来城乗の節、黒田兵庫殿先手よりに町ほど先がけて、三の丸のならしに乗あがりたる所を、矢狭間より、鑓を以て辨之助が股を突かすり者あり。辨之助甚忿て、立並びたる者どもに向ひ、「此狭間より鑓にて吾を突、鑓として見すべし」と云て、股を矢狭間にさし當て待つ。案の如く又鑓にて股を貫く。突通されながら鵜の首をひしと取て、鑓を奪取んとす。敵も取られじと引合ふ。辨之助、股の骨にあて、鵜の首よりに尺余をいて鑓を折。朋友共に、「是を見よ。鑓をとりたり」とて、少も疵を被りたる事を不言。

Having ridden into battle and laid siege to Tomiku castle, Bennosuke [Musashi] climbed the castle's ramparts some two hundred yards ahead of Kuroda Toshitaka's vanguard. There a yari, thrust through one of the castle's arrow loopholes, struck him in the waist. Infuriated, Bennosuke called out to the soldiers lined up below, "They are stabbing me from this arrow loophole here. I will show you how to get rid of it," at which point he put the upper half of his leg up against the loophole and waited. And

Though its author, Tanji Hōkin, claims that Musashi joined his father in Nakatsu and entered the service of **Kuroda Yoshitaka** (1546–1604) is contested by some, there is little doubt that Musashi's father, Muni, did indeed live in Nakatsu at this time, as his name is mentioned in the local records of the Kuroda clan (see Musashi's Father). Going by what Hōkin is saying, it seems that Muni had left the castle town of Takamori and joined his lord, Kuroda Yoshitaka, in Nakatsu, the seat of the Kuroda headquarters.

Unless Musashi had completely fallen out with his father (which is contradicted by the *Bushū denraiki*, as well as the *Numata kaki*) it is unlikely that, at the tender age of sixteen, Musashi should have ended up fighting among the western forces, in other words, that he fought opposite none other than his own father, who took part in the Battle of Sekigahara under Yoshitaka's son, Kuroda Nagamasa (1568–1623). Nor is there any evidence to suggest under whom he might have done so.

If Musashi had indeed been fighting among the ranks of one of Mitsunari's allies, why should he have relied with such consistency and apparent faith on the hospitality of Ogasawara Tadazane (Akashi), Nagaoka Okinaga (Kokura), and Hosokawa Tadatoshi (Kumamoto), all staunch supporters of the house of Tokugawa.

Musashi's eastern loyalties are also supported by the *Kōkō zatsuroku*, as well as the *Osaka o-jin no otomo* and the *Osaka o-jin o-ninzu tsukeoboe* (see below), which all clearly state that during the siege of Osaka castle Musashi served among the troops of Mizuno Katsunari (1564–1651), another chieftain who had chosen Ieyasu's side. It is, after all, very unlikely that Musashi would have fought on the side of the western forces during the Battle of Sekigahara and have switched to fight alongside the eastern forces in the defense of the castle.

Had Musashi indeed fought among the western forces, why should he furthermore have adopted Mikinosuke, the third son of another Ieyasu ally, Nakagawa Shimanosuke, who served Katsunari as *musha bugyō*, his Magistrate of Warriors?

* *Mikinosuke's background, by the way, is not provided by the Kōkō zatsuroku, but by an ancestral record drawn up in 1696 and submitted to the administrators of the Okuyama fiefdom in the province of Bizen by a certain Miyamoto Kōhei, head of a contingent of ashigaru of the Ikeda clan and a nephew of Miyamoto Mikinosuke.*

The reason why the former view (that he fought at Sekigahara) has become so entrenched among Musashi's modern-day fans can partly be ascribed to the Japanese novelist **Yoshikawa Eiji** (1892–1962), who in his epic novel Musashi, chose to have Musashi fight—and taste the bitter but cathartic experience of defeat—among Ishida Mitsunari's allies. One reason for Eiji to have done so, might well have been to heighten dramatical tension. To have Musashi fight on the losing side provided the novelist with far more scope for character development than him being among the victors.

It was, of course, the events in Musashi's personal life—his troubled relationship with his father, the ritual suicide of his first adopted son in the wake of the demise of his lord, Honda Tadatoki, and the death of his illegitimate daughter—that really determined the personal development of this battle-hardened warrior, and in ways far more profound than any defeat in battle could ever be.

The Siege of Osaka Castle

One of the most insightful documents relating to Musashi's whereabouts during the **siege of Osaka castle** is the *Kōkō zatsuroku*. Its author was Matsudaira Kunzan (1697–1783), a Confucianist scholar-warrior who was born in Nagoya and, at the age of twenty, entered the service of Tokugawa Tsugutomo, then lord of the fiefdom of Owari (in today's Aichi prefecture).

In 1743 Kunzan was appointed *kakimono bugyō*, the magistrate in charge of the fiefdom's immense archive (which comprised some 3700 documents), a post he was to occupy for the next thirty-eight years. Kunzan's intimate knowledge of the Owari archive that he built up in the course of his career gives considerable credence to his claim that during the Osaka campaign Musashi was fighting among the troops of Mizuno Katsunari (1564–1651):

大坂の時、水野日向守か手に付、三間ほとの志ない のさし物に、釈迦者仏法之為知者、我者兵法之為知 者と書れる。よき覚ハなし、何方にて有れん橋の上 にて、大木刀を持、雑人を橋の左右へなぎ伏れる様 子、見事なりと、人々誉れる。

During the siege of Osaka castle, Musashi, who was fighting with the troops of Mizuno Hyūga no Kami [Katsunari], carried a five-yard long banner on which in bold characters was written the slogan: "Men from the realm of Shakya knew and practiced the laws of Buddha; we know and practice the laws of heihō." I do not remember exactly where it was, but at one stage he was standing on a bridge, brandishing his long bokutō, and being cheered on, he cast the enemy troops off the bridge left and right.

Where the *Kōkō zatsuroku* isn't clear about the precise place and time of the event it describes, an excerpt from the *Mizuno Katsunari oboegaki*, the personal diaries of Mizuno

Katsunari, helps us to give the described events a time and place. Casting his mind back to the days leading up to the summer siege of Osaka castle, Katsunari recalls how:

片山の山から後藤軍を下へ追い崩し、道筋両側は深田にて、田の中に小さき石橋あり、先に拙者（勝成）二番に中山勘解由、三番に水野美作守、四番目に村瀬左馬、それを乗り越すと、本多左京の軍勢が追い崩され、その橋の際まで逃げかかってきたので、右四人の者、馬より降り槍を取って突き掛かり、敵を退け、藤井寺まで進撃した。

Driving down one flank of the mountain we pursued and crushed the Gotō forces and since both sides of the path were deep with mud, there was a small stone bridge amid the rice paddies. I was the first to mount the bridge, followed by Nakayama Kageyu, Mizuno Katsutoshi, and Murase Saba, and passing the bridge, we found that the forces of Honda Sakyō had been pushed back and had fled into the paddies flanking the bridge, upon which we dismounted from our horses and taking our lances, we pursued the enemy all the way back to Fujiidera.

It follows with near certainty that the *Kōkō zatsuroku* relates to the fighting during the summer campaign, which reached its climax during the first days of Juni, 1615. On 2 June, Katsunari's troops (which were part of a Tokugawa force of some thirty-eight thousand troops advancing on Osaka castle from Yamato Province) were intercepted by a vanguard of some three thousand men under the command of **Gotō Mototsugu** (1560–1615) at a place called Dōmyōji, some ten miles southwest of Osaka. Heavy fighting ensued in which Mototsugu was eventually killed and Katsunari's men prevailed.

Not surprisingly, being a record describing Katsunari's own feats and those of his clan members, the *Mizuno Katsunari oboegaki* only mentions the main participants in the battle. Naturally, they would have been leading large numbers of troops over the bridge in their pursuit of the enemy. Knowing that Musashi was one of the ten mounted guards attached to the seventeen-year-old Katsutoshi, it is safe to assume that the events as described by the *Kōkō zatsuroku* are those that took place on the bridge near Dōmyōji on 2 June 1615.

Indeed, it may well have been Nakayama Kageyu, the second retainer to follow Kagekatsu, whose recollections were passed down to his sons and their sons to finally be recorded by Matsudaira Kunzan when he visited Kageyu's descendants to record their history. It was among the archives of the Nakayama clan, after all, that one of the two roll calls (the *Osaka o-jin no otomo*) carrying Musashi's name was discovered (see below).

Oddly enough, while the popular view (especially in the West) is that Musashi fought on the side of the Toyotomi forces there are no historical records to support such a view. Perhaps chiefly to blame is again Yoshikawa Eiji, who as stated above, had cast Musashi on the side of the western (losing) forces of **Ishida Mitsunari** during the decisive Battle of Sekigahara (1600). As stated above, there is no record to support Eiji's scenario.

Eiji might have based this version of events on the knowledge that, in order to raise enough troops, the Toyotomi generals mobilized more than a hundred thousand *rōnin*, and since Musashi was a *rōnin* of sorts, his desire to cast Musashi on the losing side might have seemed justified. Having accepted that Musashi fought against Ieyasu's forces at Sekigahara it was only logical to assume that he did the same during the siege of Osaka castle.

This, however, is to ignore evidence to the contrary. And in contrast to the above view, there is ample and sound evidence that Musashi fought on the side of the Tokugawa forces under the command of Mizuno Katsunari (1564–1651). Apart from his appearance in the *Kōkō zatsuroku*, Musashi's name also appears on a roll call of men who fought under Katsunari titled *Osaka o-jin no otomo*. This record was rediscovered in 1984 among the possessions of a certain Nakayama Fumio (Nagoya), a direct descendant of Nakayama Shigemori (Shōgen), who was one of Katsunari's chief retainers.

It is believed, by the way, that during the Kan'ei era (1624–29) Musashi visited Mizuno Katsunari at his stronghold of Fukuyama castle (see Fukuyama castle). During his visit, he stayed at the *yashiki* of Nakayama Shigemori, who held a banquet in honor of his guest. A stone in the garden became Musashi's favorite place to sit while sojourning at Shigemori's *yashiki*. Though Shigemori's *yashiki* has long since been destroyed, the stone has been moved to the precincts of the Bingo Go-kuni shrine, situated on the castle ground's northern perimeter, where it graces the temple grounds. It is now known as the **Musashi Meisō Ishi** (Musashi's Meditative Stone).

The *Osaka o-jin no otomo* is not the only roll call to mention Musashi's name in connection to the siege. A similar roll call, kept among the archives of Fukuyama castle, confirms that Musashi was one among the 230 mounted warriors (in addition to some 4300 warriors on foot) mobilized under Katsunari's command. The roll call, titled *Osaka o-jin o-ninzu tsukeoboe*, originally was among the papers of the Oba, a clan of Mizuno retainers from Fukuyama. Today, two copies, one drafted in 1752, the other in 1818, are still kept in the **Kagami Yagura**, the castle's eastern turret, and both have been authored by a certain Oba Heiba.

Moreover, not only does the *Osaka o-jin o-ninzu tsukeoboe* mention that Musashi was among Katsunari's mounted warriors, it explicitly states that Musashi was the fourth among a group of ten mounted warriors attached to none other than "Sakushū-sama", the honorary name of Katsunari's son, **Mizuno Katsutoshi**. Two men among the remaining nine are marked as "taking part as *rōnin*", whereas no such label is put on Musashi.

Finally, as pointed out above, it was following the siege of Osaka castle, that Musashi adopted his first son, Mikinosuke. That much is borne out by an ancestral record drawn up in 1696 and submitted to the administrators of the Okayama fiefdom in the province of Bizen by a certain Miyamoto Kōhei, a nephew of Mikinosuke and head of a contingent of *ashigaru* of Ikeda Masakoto (1645–1700), the master of Okayama castle, on a stipend of two-hundred-and-fifty *koku*.

Tracing back his family's ancestry, Kōhei claims that Mikinosuke was in fact the third son of Nakagawa Shimanosuke. Next to nothing is known about Lord Shimanosuke, except that he was a descendant of the lord of Nakagawabara castle in the province of Ise and that at some stage he entered the service of Mizuno Katsunari. Like Musashi, Shimanosuke, too, joined Katsunari in battle during the siege of Osaka castle. He did so as a *musha bugyō*, or Magistrate of Warriors, and it is almost certain that he lost his life in the siege, for he disappears from the records in the wake of the battle.

The Shimabara Rebellion

The Shimabara rebellion, so called after the peninsula on which it played out, was the last serious military conflict to upset the centrally imposed order of the Edo Bakufu. Chief cause of the rebellion was the harsh regime of the local *daimyō*, Matsukura Shigehari, who imposed such heavy taxes on the already severely impoverished populace that many simply starved. The rebellion was led by a certain Amakusa Shiro, the son of a retainer of the Christian *daimyō*, Konishi Yukinaga.

Amakusa Shiro was also a Christian, and so were most of the rebels, who at the peak of the rebellion numbered more than twenty thousand. Among them were a considerable number of *rōnin*, masterless samurai, but most of them were simple peasants, who had been joined by their womenfolk and children.

Shiro and his fellow rebels had ensconced themselves in **Hara castle**, which had been standing empty for several years. Having erupted on 17 December 1637, the first attempts to suppress the rebellion followed within weeks. They were undertaken by the governor of Nagasaki, Sakakibara Motonao, but his forces, only a few thousand strong, suffered a crushing defeat and had to retreat to Nagasaki.

The governor now called in the help of the Bakufu, and it was on its orders that the local military clans raised a force of well over a hundred thousand troops, including some six thousand raised by the Ogasawara. Yet in spite of their overwhelming strength (and in spite of help from the Dutch, who fired more than four hundred rounds into the stronghold from one of their ships) it took the Bakufu troops up until 15 April before the stronghold finally fell. More than ten thousand Bakufu troops died in the course of the siege, but all the rebels, including women and children, were killed following the castle's fall.

The Shimabara Rebellion was the last time Musashi saw action on the battlefield. Though Mizuno Katsunari also took part in the rebellion's suppression, this time Musashi rode into battle under Ogasawara Tadazane, the *daimyō* of the Kokura fief and the lord of Musashi's son, Iori. Yet, as in the siege of Osaka castle, Musashi was not part of the common troops but was assigned as part of an escort to Tadazane's son, Nagatsugu. The *Bushū denraiki*, describes how:

始終、鎧は着し玉はず、純子の廣袖の胴着を着し、脇指をに腰さし、五尺杖をつき、信州の馬の側らに居らる。城乗の時、賊徒石を抛つ。馬前に來る石を、「石がまいる」と言葉をかて、五尺杖にてつき戻し、落城に及んでは、例の薙刀にて數人薙伏られしと也。

From start to finish Musashi was at Lord Nagatsugu's side, never putting on a harness but simply wearing a silk damask wide-sleeved undergarment, and tucking into his belt two daggers, while leaning on a five-foot wooden staff. During the castle's siege the rebels threw down stones, but Musashi leapt in front of the horse and, shouting "beware of the stones," fended them off with his staff. And when the castle finally fell he slew countless rebels with his halberd.

Though Hōkin makes no mention of it, it is widely believed that Musashi was seriously wounded during the **siege of Hara castle**. This is also borne out by a letter written shortly after the suppression of the rebellion and addressed to Arima Naozumi, the lord of Nobeoka castle in the province of Hyūga, in which Musashi mentions that he was hit by two rocks.

That Musashi had not forgotten the time he had fought alongside Katsunari's son during the fierce battle at Dōmyōji in the runup to the siege of Osaka castle, is borne out by the *Sōkyū sama o-degatari*, which describes how in response to criticism at the clamorous arrival of Katsunari's troops during the siege of Hara castle:

宮本武蔵という者是を聞き、我先年、日向守殿家に
これあり、彼軍立よく知れり、凡慮の及ばざる大将
なり、各評判の及ぶ処にあらず。

Miyamoto Musashi remarked that he had ridden into battle under Lord Katsunari some years ago and that he was well acquainted with his manner of dispersing the troops, that he was a commander who exceeded the understanding of commoners, and that his style of leadership was beyond reproach.

The **Shimabara Rebellion** was also the first—and only—time Musashi was joined by his son, Iori (see Musashi's Children). Not a warrior like his father, he probably served Tadazane in a civil capacity, safely behind the battle lines. Yet it seems Iori was of great use, for the *Harima kagami* claims that he "rendered distinguished services to his lordship" in the course of the battle, in reward for which his stipend was increased to three thousand *koku*, and that he was finally raised to the rank of senior retainer.

The Missing Battles

Writing his life's work, the *Gorin no sho*, in old age, Musashi did not touch on the battles in which he had participated during his active military career, preferring to limit himself to the statement that he had engaged in more than sixty duels by the time he had reached the age of twenty-nine. However, we do know that Musashi spent much of his life on the field of battle, for in a letter to Sakazaki Naizen, Hosokawa Tadatoshi's head of pages, he clearly states that:

若年より軍場へ出候事以上六度にて、其内四度は、其
場におゐて拙者より先ヲ懸候者、一人も無之候。其段
はあまねく何も存知之事にて、尤證據も有之候。乍然
此儀は以全く身上之申立に仕にては無之候。

From a young age I have, in all, gone into battle some six times, four times out of which I was in the absolute vanguard. This is widely known, and of course there is also proof of it. However, it is not at all with a view to advance my social position that I mention this.

Sadly, today, though it is indeed widely known, much of the proof that undoubtedly existed in Musashi's day, has been covered by the dust of time. Nevertheless, since it has been established that Musashi took part in the siege of **Tomiku castle**, the siege of Osaka castle, and the suppression of the Shimabara Rebellion, it follows that, if he is right in his claim (and there is no reason to believe he is not), Musashi participated in three more battles. The question that remains, then, is: in what other three battles did Musashi participate?

Since the siege of Tomiku castle was only part of a much larger campaign, involving a string of sieges and pitched battles, it is very possible that the three remaining battles in which Musashi fought were three of the many battles that were part of Kuroda Yoshitaka's (1546–1604) campaign to bring Kyushu under Tokugawa control. If so, it was in the course of these fierce battles over a period of many months that the young Musashi was able to hone the fighting skills he had learned from his father in Miyamoto and his uncle Dōrin in the latter's small temple near Hirafuku village.

Another scenario is that Musashi fought his remaining three battles under Mizuno Katsunari. Since Musashi served under Katsunari during the summer campaign of Osaka castle, it is quite possible, almost logical, that Musashi had also fought under Katsunari during the winter campaign. And why should he not have also taken part in Katsunari's assault on the castles of

Gifu and Ōgaki in the run-up to the Battle of Sekigahara (1600)? Indeed, there is good reason to believe that the Bukōden is referring to just that when it mentions the siege of Gifu castle in connection to Musashi.

If Masanaga is indeed suggesting that Musashi fought under Katsunari in the siege of Gifu (and Ōgaki?) castle, he leaves us with another conundrum. For in the same passage he mentions the siege of **Fushimi castle**, which, after all, was besieged by the western forces. Indeed, it was Ishida Mitsunari's unprovoked attack on Fushimi castle, which was being held by the trusty Tokugawa ally, Torii Mototada, that gave Ieyasu the reason he needed for a final confrontation between his forces and those of his western adversaries.

It was in the run-up to that confrontation on the plains of the old barrier of Sekigahara that, on 28 September, Ieyasu's troops laid siege of Gifu castle. If Musashi did indeed participate in the siege of Fushimi castle, as well as the siege of Gifu castle, he would have had to change sides within the space of only one month, which would have made him a bit of a turncoat, to say the least. Such behavior, though not uncommon in his time, simply does not fit Musashi's temperament, nor does it sit well with the long string of Musashi's Benefactors, all of whom were staunch Tokugawa supporters.

Interestingly, the wording of the *Bukō-den*, which merely states that Musashi "set foot in Fushimi castle" (*Fushimi-jō wo fumu*), might be constructed to mean that Musashi was part of the **Torii Mototada's** defending force. However, the castle fell in the attack, and Mototada and many of his men were killed. Musashi, then, must have been one of the few lucky ones to escape with his skin. This, in itself, is not impossible, but one would at least expect one mention of such a feat by the many chroniclers of his day.

The truth, of course, is that we do not know. As long as we remain deprived of vital sources such as the *Osaka o-jin no otomo* and the *Osaka o-jin o-ninzu tsukeoboe*, we simply cannot establish in what remaining battles Musashi participated and what his exact role was. What is certain is that, very much like his deadly duels, he had fought most of his battles (with the exception of the Shimabara Rebellion) by the age of thirty-one (1615), for by then Japan had been fully pacified.

MUSASHI'S BENEFACTORS

Kuroda Yoshitaka

To find out more about **Kuroda Yoshi-taka**, the southern warlord whom by dint of being the lord of Musashi's father, Muni, was Musashi's first host of sorts during his youth, we first have to turn to Musashi's proclivities in old age. The *Bushū denraiki* describes how:

武州、老年に至り、命終の所を可極と被存立。古郷
と云、武勇と云、黒田の御家か、又は、兵法数寄に
てある間、細川の家かに可致とて、先筑前に被下。

In old age, Musashi began to think about a place where he could spend the end of his life. Thinking about his hometown and military prowess it was the house of Kuroda that sprang to mind first, but when it came to the elegant pursuits of heihō, it was the house of Hosokawa that was foremost in his mind. Preoccupied with these thoughts he decided to at least make his way to the province of Chikuzen.

We now know why it was that Musashi first thought of the Kuroda, for it is now clear that Musashi's father, Muni, had entered the service of **Kuroda Toshitaka** before the Battle of Sekigahara (see Musashi's Father). When Toshitaka died in 1596, Muni entered the service of Toshitaka's brother Yoshitaka, whose headquarters of Nakatsu castle still crowns this otherwise somewhat uninspiring coastal town. From the *Bushū denraiki*, written in 1815 by Tanji Hōkin, we also now know that not long after Muni had moved down to Kyushu, Musashi decided to seek out his father at his new home in the port town of Nakatsu (see Musashi's Places).

Little is known about Musashi's time in Nakatsu. Musashi at this time was only in his late teens, and while his father might have been a fencing instructor to the Kuroda clan, it is not likely that a boy of Musashi's age would have had been in a position to establish any personal rapport with a *daimyō* of Yoshitaka's stature. yet it is clear from the *Bushū denraiki* that he did participate in the siege of Tomiku castle, only one of a string of sieges through which Yoshitaka brought northern Kyushu under Tokugawa control (see Musashi's Battles).

Musashi probably stayed with his father until 1605, when, at the age of twenty-one, he went up to Kyoto to seek out the Yoshioka brothers and challenge them to a duel. From that point onwards, until Musashi shows up in himeji to seek out Honda Tadamasa, it is unclear where Musashi exactly stayed, for it was during this period, when he was in his twenties, that the swordsman traveled the country extensively on his many *musha shugyō*. And while he stayed at certain places for extended periods of time (Kyoto, Edo, Kokura, Kitsuki), it was only later in life, when he sought to settle down, that he accepted the invitation of powerful *daimyō* (with the means to support him for extended periods of time) to be their guest.

Honda Tadamasa

In the wake of the summer campaign of Osaka castle, Musashi visited Himeji, where he met with **Honda Tadamasa** (1575–1631). Since the Kuroda had left for Kyushu Himeji castle had become the headquarters of the newly established fief of Himeji. Its first *daimyō*, Ikeda Terumasa (1565–1613), had taken up residence in the wake of the Battle of Sekigahara. He had been succeeded by his son, Toshitaka (1584–1616). When the latter died his son was still only seven years old, so that the Bakufu decided to demote the Ikeda to the Tottori fief in Kyushu and make Honda Tadamasa the new *daimyō* of Himeji.

There is good reason to believe that Musashi had already met Tadamasa during the summer campaign of Osaka castle. During the storming of the castle, Lord Tadamasa had been in command of the second eastern phalanx, immediately behind the troops of Mizuno Katsunari. At that time Tadamasa's headquarters had still been at **Kuwana castle**, on the Bay of Ise. With Tadamasa's new appointment, Musashi found the opportunity to settle in the province where his mother was still living and to provide a future for his adopted son, Mikinosuke (see Musashi's Children).

The *Bisan hōkan* claims that Tadamasa even sought to hire Musashi following a match between the swordsman and one of his retainers by the name of Miyake Gundayū (see Musashi's Bouts):

忠政、武藏を召して臣事せよと。武藏辞して云、吾志望あり、藩士となるの意なし。遂に二百石を給して、藩士の子弟を・授せしむ。

Tadamasa summoned Musashi and proposed that Musashi enter his service. But Musashi declined, saying, "I am an ambitious man and do not wish to become a retainer." In the end, Lord Tadamasa granted Musashi a stipend of two hundred koku and made him instruct his young clansmen.

It was almost certainly with Tadamasa's consent that Musashi's son entered the service of Tadamasa's son, Tadatoki, who at the time was still only twenty-one years old. Tadamasa, after all, had known Mikinosuke's natural father, whose castle of Nakagawabara was situated only a few miles down the coast from his former headquarters at Kuwana. Given his young age, Tadatoki had been put in control of the Nitta-*han*, another fiefdom in Harima of some ten thousand *koku* in size, although it had no castle and Tadatoki probably resided at Himeji castle.

Sadly, Tadatoki passed away In the summer of 1626. It was common practice in those days to immolate oneself on the death of one's lord, a practice called *junshi*. As tradition required, Mikinosuke did so in front of his master's grave on the sixth day following the latter's demise. He was only twenty-three years old. Had the incident happened half a century later, Mikinosuke would have been barred from following his master in death, for, in 1663, the Edo Bakufu prohibited the practice by decree.

It seems that Mikinosuke's adoptive father was not present at the heartrending ceremony, for the *Bushū denraiki* claims that Musashi was in Osaka at the time. In fact, though Musashi would have spent much of his time in Harima, it is not clear where exactly he stayed, as it is not clear either where his son's master resided.

Ogasawara Tadazane

Ogasawara Tadazane (1596–1667) is the lord with whom Musashi spent the longest and the happiest time. It was probably again through Honda Tadamasa's offices that, in 1626, not long after his son had followed his master in death, Musashi accepted Tadazane's invitation to come and live in Akashi and assist him with the construction of the new castle town. With his experience of siege warfare, Musashi served as an adviser to the *zōei bugyō*, the construction magistrate in charge of the whole project. Recognizing the warrior's artistic qualities Tadazane also put Musashi in charge of the design of the castle gardens (see Musashi's Places).

Like Tadamasa, Tadazane was a *fūdai*, or vassal *daimyō*, whose role it was to guard the Bakufu against conspiracies by any of the *tozama*, or outside *daimyō*, those who had failed to choose the side of the house of Tokugawa in the previous conflicts. Given that much of the initial resistance against the

Tokugawa had emanated from western Honshu, it was not surprising that many of the domains to the west of Akashi and Himeji were ruled by *tozama daimyō*.

It was to form a buffer against these potentially hostile *daimyō* (and as a first line of defense around Osaka and Edo castles, the centers of Bakufu power) that Ieyasu had devised the delicate distribution of fiefs by which the loyal Honda and Ogasawara clans had acquired their new domains. And it was to bolster that first line of defense that, on the specific order of Ieyasu's son and successor, Hidetada, Tadamasa was ordered to take in hand the construction of **Akashi castle** and its environs.

The foundations for the new Akashi castle were laid along the coast of the Inland Sea, right at the strategic narrow between the mainland and the island of Awaji. From there, any hostile traffic through the Straits of Akashi could be stopped before it reached Osaka. A harbor was built at **Akashi** for the small fleet of ships that would police the straits, while a newly laid out castle town was erected to house all the retainers, mariners, merchants, and artisans who in one way or other served the young lord of Akashi castle.

Ogasawara Tadazane, of course, was also the lord of Musashi's second adopted son, Iori (see Musashi's Children). Iori accompanied Tadazane to Kyushu following the latter's promotion to the fief of Kokura, serving a succession of Ogasawara notables, and eventually rising to the rank of chief retainer on a stipend of five thousand *koku* (see Musashi's Children). Musashi, too, was to join his son in Kokura, although he did so after a string of visits to other places, and would later in life move to Kumamoto.

Mizuno Katsunari

Mizuno Katsunari (1564–1651) was born at Kariya castle, in the province of Mikawa. The strands of his clan were closely intertwined with those of the Tokugawa (then still called Matsudaira), who had their headquarters in nearby Okazaki castle. His aunt was none other than Ieyasu's mother, making Katsunari Ieyasu's direct cousin. Katsunari had made his career in the Tokugawa ranks and had fought in numerous battles under Ieyasu, including the famous battles of Komaki and Nagakute (1584), the only time Ieyasu and Hideyoshi ever confronted each other on the field of battle.

It seems that the young Katsunari was possessed of the same fierce temperament as Musashi, for it was during the battle of Nagakute that the young warrior landed himself in trouble when he killed one of his father's retainers in a fit of anger and was expelled from Mikawa Province for a while. It was partly through the intervention of his cousin, Ieyasu, that relations with his father were restored. Over the following years, he continued to serve Ieyasu, most conspicuously so in the run-up to the Battle of Sekigahara, when he distinguished himself in the sieges of Gifu and Ōgaki castles.

Exactly how Katsunari and Musashi first met is unclear. The first document to suggest a relationship—if not outright friendship—between Musashi and Katsunari is a recently discovered copy of Musashi's *Heidō kagami* addressed to none other than Katsunari himself. Today only copies of the *Heidō kagami* exist, though their provenance is disputed by some Japanese historians.

One of the documents is dated "an auspicious day," in the twelfth month of the thirteenth year of Keichō (January 1609). This means that Musashi had met and befriended Katsunari by the time he was only twenty-five. This in itself makes sense, since at that age was still living in Edo developing his Enmei school of swordsmanship. By then, Musashi had already made a name for himself by defeating the famed Yoshioka brothers (though this, in turn, is disputed by the *Yoshioka-den*), and it is not unimaginable that Katsunari had somehow met and practiced with Musashi during his many visits to Edo.

This scenario also provides us with a clue as to how Musashi came to serve Katsunari during the siege of Osaka castle. If Katsunari had come to know Musashi in **Edo** and had been impressed with his skills, it is easier to understand that he would have chosen him to serve as his son's guard during such a dangerous campaign a few years later.

it must have been their similarly fierce disposition that drew the two warriors together. A man of high birth, Katsunari was very much Musashi's senior, but the great trust he put in the western warrior was revealed when, in 1615, during the summer campaign against Osaka castle, he appointed Musashi as an attendant to his son Katsutoshi.

More proof of the close relation between Musashi and the house of Mizuno came shortly afterward, when Musashi, who had no natural sons of his own, adopted the third (and possibly also the fourth) son of Nakagawa Shimanosuke. Shimanosuke was the lord of Nakagawabara castle in the province of Ise, who had served Katsunari as *musha bugyō*, the Magistrate of Warriors, during the siege of Osaka castle, a siege in which he died.

Yet another document to support the theory that there was a close relationship between Musashi and Katsunari is he *Sōkyū sama o-degatari*, which describes how, in response to criticism at the clamorous arrival of Katsunari's troops during the siege of Hara castle:

宮本武蔵という者是を聞き、我先年、日向守殿家に
これあり、彼軍立よく知れり、凡慮の及ばざる大将
なり、各評判の及ぶ処にあらず。

Miyamoto Musashi remarked that he had ridden into battle under Lord Katsunari some years earlier and that he was well acquainted with his manner of dispersing the troops, that he was a commander who exceeded the though of commoners, and that his style of leadership was beyond reproach.

It is believed that during the Kan'ei era (1624–29) Musashi visited Mizuno Katsunari at his castle at Fukuyama (see Musashi's Places). During his visit, he stayed at the *yashiki* of Nakayama Shigemori, who held a banquet in honor of his guest. A stone in the garden had become Musashi's favorite place to sit while sojourning at Shigemori's *yashiki*. Though Shigemori's *yashiki* has long since been destroyed, the stone has been moved to the precincts of the Bingo Go-kuni shrine, situated on the castle ground's northern perimeter, where it graces the temple grounds under the name of Musashi Meisō Ishi (Musashi's Meditative Stone).

Matsudaira Katsutaka

The *Bushū denraiki* describes how,

寛永の比、武州、松平出雲守殿の家にあり。雲州の
家頼に多力の兵法者あり。雲州、彼と武州との勝負
を望まる。

In the era of Kan'ei [1624–44] Musashi stayed at the house of lord Matsudaira Izumo no Kami [Katsutaka]. Among the retainers of lord Naomasa, there were a great number of heihōsha, and his lordship wished to see them have a match with Musashi.

It goes on to describe in great detail how Musashi won the match hands-down within moments. Disappointed with the outcome his lordship then takes up a *bokutō* to test his strength on the swordsman himself.

Born in 1589, Matsudaira Katsutaka was only five years younger than Musashi and known for his great love of swordsmanship. He was the son of one of Ieyasu's most senior vassals and had held a string of important positions within the Bakufu. In the spring of 1634, he had moved down to the province of Iyo, on the island of Shikoku, to take up temporary residence on the grounds of **Iyo Matsuyama castle**. The former lord of Matsuyama castle had passed away and the Bakufu decided that henceforth the Matsuyama domain was to be governed by a member of the Matsudaira, a clan from which the Tokugawa descended. It was Katsutaka's duty to prepare the *hikiwatashi*, the castle's smooth transfer from one clan to another.

The *Bushū denraiki* is the only original source to mention this encounter. To be true to the text, it only speaks of Matsudaira Izumo no Kami. This has led a number of historians to believe that Musashi was the guest of **Matsudaira Naomasa** (1601–66), the grandson of Tokugawa Ieyasu, and the lord of Matsue castle. Matsue castle, after all, is located in what once was the province of Izumo, leading them to assume that the honorific title of "Izumo no Kami" must have referred to its master, Matsudaira Naomasa. This, however, is to ignore the fact that it was Katsutaka who bore the title of Izumo no Kami, and not Naomasa (whose honorific title was Dewa no Kami). Katsutaka's clan, moreover, was related to the Ogasawara (Tadazane's fourth son was adopted by Katsutaka's oldest brother), and it is very plausible that he and Musashi met at Akashi or Kokura castle.

Another strong indication that the event was not staged at Matsue but at Matsuyama is the fact that the same record states that Musashi "stayed at the house of Lord Matsudaira

Izumo no Kami" (*Matsudaira Izumo no Kami no ie ni ari*), rather than at his castle, which would logically have been the case had he been the guest of Lord Naomasa, the master of Matsue castle. If, therefore, Musashi's host was Katsutaka and not Naomasa, the match would have been held somewhere in the vicinity of Matsuyama castle, where Katsukata would have stayed in an official accommodation, rather than at the lord's palace within the castle grounds.

Hosokawa Tadatoshi

The connections between Musashi and **Hosokawa Tadatoshi** (1586–1641) went all the way back to the swordsman's duel with Sasaki Kojirō on Ganryū Island. Tadatoshi, at that time, was still the master of Moji castle, a few miles northeast of Kokura. In the redistribution of fiefs in the wake of the Battle of Sekigahara, the Kuroda had been promoted to the fief of Fukuoka, and Tadatoshi's father, Tadaoki (1563–1646), had been promoted to their former fief of Nakatsu. Tadaoki, however, had not moved his headquarters to Nakatsu castle, but had instead taken up residence in Kokura castle and bestowed Moji castle on his son.

It is quite likely that Tadatoshi was actively involved in the organization of the contest. Tadatoshi, who was in his late twenties at the time of the duel, is reputed to have been an avid practitioner of the martial arts. Moreover, given that, according to the *Bukōden*, Kojirō was one of the Hosokawa clan's fencing instructors, Tadatoshi naturally would have had a keen interest in the duel's outcome. Indeed, he may well have practiced the art of fencing under Kojirō. If this is true, it seems all the more remarkable that Tadatoshi took such a neutral stance.

At the same time, the *Bushū denraiki* claims that Tadatoshi knew Musashi well. It also claims that the event was witnessed by Tadatoshi himself. The *Bukōden*, by contrast, only makes mention of what it refers to as Lord Tadaoki's *kenshi*, or "inspectors." No mention is made of Tadatoshi himself. It even mentions that some sources claim that Musashi was chased off the island by Hosokawa retainers who were riled by the outcome of the bout. Though these may have been Kojirō's *deshi*, it seems unlikely since, according to its author, Toyoda Masanaga, Tadaoki had strictly forbidden anyone to observe or participate in the duel.

Be this as it may, as quoted above, it was undoubtedly the Hosokawa's "elegant pursuits of *heihō*" that made Musashi decide in old age to take up Tadatoshi's offer to come and stay in Kumamoto. Written by a retainer of one of Tadatoshi's close vassals, the *Bukōden* describes the delicate negotiations that preceded Musashi's move to Kumamoto.

Like Musashi, Hosokawa Tadatoshi was by now also advanced in years, and he had come a long way since he had witnessed the duel between Musashi and Sasaki Kojirō on Ganryū Island. As the third son of **Hosokawa Tadaoki** (1563–1646) he had been bound to remain lord of Moji castle, a minor figure in the larger feudal scheme of things. But when his eldest brother was disinherited, it was Tadatoshi, and not his second eldest brother (who would later join Toyotomi Hideyori at Osaka castle out of resentment), who was chosen to succeed his father in 1620 and become master of Kokura castle and the clan's fiefdom in Buzen.

Unprepared though he was, Tadatoshi acquitted himself well—so well that, in 1632, he was promoted to the Kumamoto fiefdom, a vast estate of more than five-hundred-thousand *koku* in the neighboring province of Higo. This meant that the Kokura fiefdom was free to be bestowed on someone else, and it so happened that the Bakufu chose

Ogasawara Tadazane to be the new lord of the Kokura fief-dom. It had been Tadatoshi's promotion to the Kumamoto fief, then, that enabled the promotion of Ogasawara Tadazane to the fief in Kokura, and thereby Musashi's (and his son's) final move to Kyushu.

MUSASHI'S PLACES

Miyamoto Village

Miyamoto Musashi's birthplace according to the Mimasaka-*setsu*, or the Mimasaka tradition, is the small village of **Miyamoto** (see Musashi's Birthplace). It was originally situated in the Yoshino district of the province of Mimasaka. Today, it is part of the village of Ōhara, in the district of Aida in Okayama prefecture).

In Musashi's time, the village of Miyamoto was hidden among the mountains, with only a few traffic arteries to connect it to the rest of Japan: the Yoshino River and the Inaba Kaidō, the ancient highroad that ran from the town of Tottori on the Sea of Japan to the magnificent castle town of Himeji.

Miyamoto village was guarded by Takeyama castle, which stood on the eponymous hill overlooking both Miyamoto and Hara village. Master of **Takeyama castle** when Musashi was born was Shinmen Munetsura, the brother of Musashi's natural mother, Omasa, who had died when giving birth to Musashi. Today, not a stone of Takeyama castle remains, but looking up from Miyamoto, one can vividly imagine how splendid it must have looked on its lofty crest.

One of the major attractions of Miyamoto village is, of course, the place of Musashi's birth. Sadly, the large *yashiki*, or mansion, with its thick thatched roof in the *kayabuki* tradition was destroyed by fire during the middle of the twentieth century. But a nice description of the house has been preserved in the *Tōsakushi*, a topography compiled in 1815 by Masaki Teruo, who served Matsudaira Yasuchika, the *daimyō* of the Tsuyama fief in Mimasaka. Teruo acted as an advisor and instructor in the Kōshū-*ryū*, a school of martial arts connected to the house of Takeda Shingen (1521–73):

三十間四方、石垣は寛永十五年天草一揆のとき、公儀より命令があって取崩すと云々。大木の槻の木がある。周囲二丈七尺の太さである。荒牧大明神にある巨木と雌雄であるという。

Miyamoto Musashi's yashiki occupies an area of some three thousand square yards. It is said that, in the fifteenth year of Kanei [1638], at the time of the Shimabara Rebellion, the stone wall that surrounded it was demolished by order of the authorities. It stood in the shade of a tall zelkova with a circumference of some twenty-seven feet, which can compete with the old tree on the premise of the Aramaki Daimyō shrine [today's Sanomo shrine].

During the 20th century, a new house with a tiled roof in the *irimoya* tradition has been erected where the old **Miyamoto** *yashiki* once stood. In addition, a memorial stone in its garden still marks the place where the *yashiki* once stood.

Musashi Shrine

Though the local **Musashi shrine** was erected long after the famed swordsman had died, it celebrates, in good Shintō tradition, his life and spirit. It is, therefore, worth a visit, if only because it is a tranquil hike up the densely wooded mountain.

The shrine is locally known for being the site of what are claimed to be the graves of Hirata Muni, his wife Omasa, and most controversially, the grave of Miyamoto Musashi himself.

It is easiest to dispel the notion that Musashi's remains would rest at this site, however close it might be to his birthplace of Miyamoto (although even that is contested by some). Of all the records connected to Musashi, there is not one that claims his remains were brought back from Kumamoto (where he definitely died), all the way back to the village of Miyamoto. It is most likely, therefore, that the shrine was built during the Musashi boom in the wake of the publication of Yoshikawa Eiji's novel.

More difficult it is with the grave of Hirata Muni. The *Tōsakushi* (1851) mentions an old tombstone among the Jigami hills, above the old family *yashiki* in Miyamoto, and assumes it must mark Muni's grave. Its author, Masaki Teruo, came to this conclusion by studying the family lineage of the Hirata clan, which mentions the same date as inscribed on the gravestone. Intriguingly, the Buddhist name that is engraved on the stone reads *Shingen-in Ichinyo Dōni* (真源院一如道仁居). That exact same name is also mentioned in records of the Hirata family lineage. There, however, it is connected to a certain Buni (武二), and not Muni (無二).

The gravestone, then, does not seem to mark the grave of Muni—who almost certainly died in Kyushu, probably in Kitsuki—but that of Muni's father. That would make the most sense chronologically, for the date of death on the withered stone (as well as that mentioned in the Hirata family lineage) reads "the eighteenth day of the fourth month of the eighth year of the Tenshō era [31 May 1580].

Kamasake Pass

Following the Inaba Kaidō eastward, one reaches the Kamasake pass, which formed the natural boundary between the provinces of Mimasaka and Harima. Musashi is believed to have crossed the pass when, following an altercation with his father at the age of nine, he left his hometown and crossed

the **Kamasaka pass** toward Hirafuku, where his stepmother, Yoshiko, had been living since her divorce from his father, Muni (see Musashi's Mother). It is not sure whether Musashi ever visited Miyamoto again after he fell out with his father, but the *Tōsakushi* claims that:

伝承によれば、宮本武蔵が武者修行に出発した時、森岩彦兵衛が中山村の鎌坂まで見送った。その時、武蔵は突いていた杖を森岩に与えて、離別を告げた。

It is said that Moriiwa Hikobei would accompany Miyamoto Musashi to the Kamazaka hills of Nakamura whenever he went on one of his musha shugyō. At such times he would give his walking cane to Moriiwa and they would say their farewell.

Halfway up the small road towards the pass is a small well that runs continuously, hence its name **ikkan Shimizu**, or "continuous clear water well." The well is marked by a small rock with a short inscription that runs: "Musashi looks back on his hometown."

At the foot of the unpaved uphill road, a *tori-i* **gate** on the left side of the road marks the beginning of a path that leads up to the Musashi shrine. A signpost near the gate claims that "though Musashi died in Kumamoto, Kyushu, his adopted son, Iori, buried his remains at the grave site of the Hirata clan for the repose of his spirit."

Hirafuku

The beautiful village of Hirafuku, straddling the Sayō River, is known as the birthplace of Musashi's stepmother, Yoshiko, of whom Musashi is believed to have been very fond. Like

Musashi's real mother Yoshiko was of noble birth. Her clan belonged to a junior line of the Akamatsu clan and Yoshiko's father, Bessho Shigeharu, had been the master of Rikan castle, which overlooked the town of Hirafuku, not far from Harima's border with Mimasaka.

Following her divorce from Muni, sometime during the 1590s, Yoshiko moved back to Harima and settled down in the village of **Hirafuku**. She remarried, this time with a member of her own clan, a man by the name of Tasumi Masahisa. The name Tasumi (rice-field dweller), suggests that he belonged to a family of farmers, although it is believed that Masahira held the position of village elder. Unlike Rikan castle, the Tasumi manor has survived the centuries.

At a loss what to do, Yoshiko entrusted the care of her son to her brother. Though once a warrior, the latter had renounced the world to dedicate himself to a life of study and meditation. Taking on the name of Dōrin, he was now living in a small Buddhist temple called the **Shōrenan**, which was set among a bamboo grove on the edge of the village. It was there that Musashi grew up and spent the rest of his youth—an experience that was to have a seminal influence on his development.

Hirafuku, in Musashi's day, was one of the stations along the Inaba Kaidō. Many warriors would pass through the village and stay at one of its taverns on their *musha shugyō*. The village of Hirafuku is also believed to have been the place where Musashi fought his first duel. Known locally as the *Miyamoto Musashi kettō no ba*, or "the place of Musashi's decisive duel," His opponent in this duel was Arima Kihei (see Musashi's Duels).

Taishi

Musashi's birthplace according to the Harima-*setsu*, or the Harima tradition, is found in today's Taishi-*machi*, on the western outskirts of Himeji city (see Musashi's Birthplace). The house where Musashi grew up is said to have stood on the western side of the **Sekkai shrine**. The shrine is dedicated to the spirit of Toneri Shinnō (676–735), an imperial prince from the Nara period, who oversaw the compilation of the *Nihon Shoki* (720), the second-oldest chronicle of Japanese history.

Though Musashi's house has long since gone, an **old well** still marks the place where Musashi (then still called Bennosuke) is said to have received his first bath, a significant event in the life of a Japanese infant. An old tree leaning heavily on two metal struts is oddly reminiscent of the old tree in Masaki Teruo's description of the Miyamoto *yashiki* in his *Tōsakushi*. Yet, unlike Teruo's *keyaki* (*Zelkova serrata*) this is the Japanese *muku* tree (*Aphanthe aspera*), which is usually found in higher altitudes.

Nakatsu

It is now clear that, after Musashi had broken up with his father and moved in with his mother, his father, Muni, had left the service of Shinmen Munesada, and entered the service of Kuroda Toshitaka (see Musashi's Father). When Toshitaka died in 1596, Muni entered the service of his brother Yoshitaka, whose headquarters of **Nakatsu castle** still crown this otherwise uninspiring coastal town.

It was around this time that Musashi decided to seek out his father in Kyushu. According to the *Bushū denraiki*, written in 1815 by Tanji Hōkin:

辨之助中津へ下リ、父が勘氣をも赦免し、父子一所
にあり。是、辨之助十七歳の時なり。

Bennosuke traveled down to Nakatsu and, having regained Muni's favor, father and son were living together again. At this time Bennosuke was seventeen years of age.

In 1600, while his great ally, Tokugawa Ieyasu, was moving against an alliance of western forces led by Ishida Mitsunari at Sekigahara, Yoshitaka launched a massive campaign to subdue northern Kyushu. Beginning with Aki and Tomiku castle, he subdued the castles of Usuki, Saiki, Tsunomure, Hinokuma, Kawaradake, and Kokura in quick succession. He was so successful that within the space of just a month he had brought under his control two complete provinces.

And it was in these fierce battles that the young Musashi was able to hone the fighting skills he had learned from his father in Miyamoto and the brother of his uncle Dōrin at the small Shōrenan temple near Hirafuku village.

Kitsuki

Kitsuki is perhaps one of the places least associated with Musashi. Yet, following his first battle experiences during Kuroda Yoshitaka's (1546–1604) campaign to subdue northern Kyushu (see Musashi's Battles), he moved from Nakatsu to Kitsuki with his father, Muni, when the latter became fencing instructor to Nagaoka (Matsui) Yasuyuki (1550–1612), the master of Kitsuki castle and Hosokawa Tadatoshi's most trusted vassal (see Musashi's Father).

Kitsuki is situated at the foot of Morie Bay, on the eastern side of the Kunisaki Peninsula, some thirty miles east from

Nakatsu in the neighboring province of Bungo. The Kitsuki fief belonged to Hosokawa Tadaoki (1563–1646), who received it in reward for siding with Tokugawa Ieyasu against Ishida Mitsunari in the run-up to the Battle of Sekigahara.

Musashi visited his father (who had now taken the Buddhist name of Munisai) again in the fall of 1612 not long after his famous duel with Sasaki Kojirō on Funa Island, a duel that had been arranged by Nagaoka Okinaga. The *Numata kaki* describes how he first found refuge at Moji castle, the then residence of Hosokawa Tadatoshi, and that:

其後武蔵を豊後へ被送遣候、石井三之丞と申馬乗に、鉄砲之共ども御附被成、道を致警護無別条豊後へ送届武蔵無二斎と申者に相渡申候由に御座候。

Afterward, Musashi was brought to the province of Bungo. He was given an escort by Ishii Mitsunojō, who secured the way with men on horseback, who were armed with muskets and ensured that Musashi arrived in Bungo unharmed. There he delivered him to the house of a man by the name of Munisai.

Once the proud headquarters of Nagaoka Okinaga, **Kitsuki castle**'s original structures have long since gone, having been dismantled during the Meiji period. Replaced by a post-war reconstruction, the castle stood on the crest of Daiyama, a hill on the northern bank of the Yasaka River and overlooked Morie Bay.

Nowadays, Kitsuki is perhaps best known for the traditional living quarters of the local samurai. These so-called **buke yashiki** (武家屋敷) stand on a hill that stretches westward from the castle. One can reach them by climbing a long stone-paved stairway of fifty-

three steps on the hill's eastern slope. Atop the hill, the narrow road is flanked by long *tsuchikabe*, the traditional plastered walls. Set in these walls are roofed gateways through which one can enter the *buke yashiki*'s artfully designed gardens. The narrow road terminates in the **Suya no Saka**, a sloping road (*saka*) at the foot of which once stood a vinegar shop (*suya*).

Most of the *bukke yashiki* in Kitsuki date back to the time the fiefdom was under the control of the Matsudaira clan, when they became masters of the domain in 1645. Yet it was in such a similar *yashiki* that Musashi once lived with his father, Muni, after the latter had entered the service of Nagaoka Okinaga during the first decade of the seventeenth century.

Tanukidani Fūdō-in

It is widely believed that, when Musashi arrived in Kyoto in 1604 to challenge the Yoshioka brothers in duel, he stayed in the small village of Ichijōji, situated at the foot of Mount Uryū, northeast of the former capital.

During his stay, he is said to have frequented a **cave** in the slope of the mountain now associated with the Tanukidani Fūdō monastery. The earliest references to the **cave** are from the middle of the Kenchō era (1249–56), when an image of Acala, one of the Five Wisdom Kings was painted onto the face of a cave. By Musashi's time, the cave had become a place of pilgrimage, especially to the *yamabushi* of Mount Hiei.

In 1718 a temple was built over the cave, hiding it under the temple's main hall. Given the steep slope, the temple was constructed in the image of the famous Kiyomizu temple, atop an elaborate wooden scaffold. Sitting on its high poles on the slopes of Mount Uryū, the Tanukidani Fūdō monastery still overlooks the northeastern outskirts of the capital.

According to legend, Musashi would meditate at the foot of a small **waterfall** near the cave. There he would silently pray to Acala. Armed with a flaming sword in his right hand and a noose in his left hand, this "immovable protector," a servant of the great Buddha, was believed to destroy all obstacles on the path towards enlightenment. It is at the foot of the waterfall that the swordsman is believed to have gained the insight that victory would not be achieved through his hatred of his enemy, but by conquering the fear and worldly passions within.

The **Tanukidani Fudō-in** is the starting point of the Oku no In Sanjū-roku Meguri, or the Tour of the Thirty-six Boys of the Inner Sanctum. Starting from a stairway marked by a red *tori-i*, a narrow path along the slopes of Mount Uryū leads along thirty-six sites with small statues of infants. The trail is better known as the Masshōgun Jizōshō Sondō (元勝軍地蔵尊道), after the Shōgun Jizō (勝軍地蔵), or the Road in honor of the True Victorious Jizō, the Battlefield Protector, who is venerated in a small temple at the summit at the end of the trail, and from which the mountain derives its popular name of Mount Shōgun.

* *The Shōgun Jizō is widely venerated in Japan by warriors, who believed that the deity would vicariously receive a warrior's injuries incurred in battle. A story in the Taiheiki (1371), for instance, describes a soldier taking refuge at the Jizō Hall of Mibu after fleeing from a battle in the capital. A priest who was*

the incarnation of the Jizō in the hall appeared and was captured by the enemy in place of the soldier.

Rendai Plain

The *Kokura hibun*, as well as the *Bushū denraiki* and the *Bukōden* agree that Musashi's first duel with the members of the Yoshioka clan (see Musashi's Duels) took place on the so-called 蓮台野, or the **Rendai plains**, situated close to Funaokayama (船岡山), a small hill on the northern outskirts of Kyoto.

The Rendai plains were known as the burial grounds of the nearby Jōhon **Rendai temple**. According to the *Honchō bunshū* the temple was built in 960 by the Heian monk Kankū of the Shingon sect to honor his deceased father and mother. During the Heian period (794–1185), Funaokayama was used as a cremation site. Thus the *Heike monogatari* describes how, having died at only twenty-three, Emperor Nijō "was carried to Funaokayama, on the other side of the Rendai plains to the northeast of the Kōryū temple."

Once a barren plain on the outskirts of the former capital, today, the Rendai plains have been swallowed up by the urban sprawl of Kyoto's Kamigyo ward. Funaokayama still rises above the sea of surrounding roofs, yet it has long since lost its sinister character, as it is now Funaokayama Park, a pleasant island of green amid Kyoto's urban sprawl.

* *Tanji Jitsuzan (1655–1708), the brother of the author of the Bushū denraiki, Tanji Hōkin, was befriended with Manzan Dōhaku (1635–1715) the abbot of the Genkōan, a monastery of the Sōtō sect situated not far from the Rendai plains and known for its beautiful interiors.*

Though it is the only record to do so, the *Koro usawa* claims the duel was instead fought at "Kitano's Shichihonmatsu," literally: "Kitano's seven pine trees," which seems to be a reference to what is still called Shichihonmatsu-*dōri*, one of Kyoto's main thoroughfares just east of the famous Kitano Tenman-gū shrine.

Sagarimatsu

The *Bushū denraiki* locates the third duel between Musashi and the members of the Yoshioka clan (see Musashi's Duels) at "Sagarimatsu, on the outskirts of Kyoto." It is a vexingly elusive designation as there are many places around the capital that are historically associated with that name.

The *Bukōden* seems to throw more light on the exact place where the ambush was staged. Although, like the *Bushū denraiki*, it follows the *Kokura hibun* in its initial description of the venue (i.e., on the outskirts of the former capital), it claims that it was at a place called Yabuzato, in the village of **Ichijōji**. When citing Musashi's account of the event to his *deshi*, Dōke Kakusaemon, it adds, in brackets, that it was "at Yabusato near the village of Ichijōji." (一乗寺村藪里にあり). Its spin-off, the *Nitenki*, sees no need for brackets, boldly stating Musashi was ambushed at "a place called Yabu no Sato Sagarimatsu of Ichijōji village, on the outskirts of the capital." (洛外一乗寺村藪の郷下り松と云う處).

In Musashi's day, Ichijōji was just a small hamlet on the capital's eastern outskirts. It was so called after the **Ichijō temple**, a Tendai sect temple built during the middle of the Heian period (794–1185). In 981 the temple is believed to have been the refuge of the Tendai monk Shūsan, when rivaling factions of the sect were fighting each other. Seven years later, the temple was visited by Emperor Enyū (959–991), but it fell into disrepair during the heavy fighting around the capital during the Two Courts Period (1333–92) and was eventually demolished.

Like the Rendai plains, it has long since been swallowed up by Kyoto's urban sprawl. The name Yabusato is less easy to trace. There is today no place in Kyoto called Yabusato or Yabu no Sato. In historical records, however, the place is regularly described as Ichjōji Yabusato. The character for *yabu* (薮) suggests that the place was known for a grove, which seems a logical place for the Yoshioka in their attempt to ambush the rival swordsman.

It is probably because of the *Bukōden*'s specific description—and in particular the popularity of the *Nitenki*—that most Japanese believe that the venue of the third duel with the Yoshioka brothers was at Ichijōji. Today, the place is set along a junction amid a sleepy suburban area, marked by two obelisk-like memorial stones set amid a small but carefully tended triangular terrace.

Musashi's duel with the Yoshioka brothers is celebrated at the nearby Hachidai shrine, which is now situated in a wooded area behind the **Shisen monastery**. Founded in 1294, the shrine owned large tracts of land, or *keidai*, in the surrounding area, including a place called Sagarimatsu.

There are three locations that qualify as the place where, according to the *Bushū denraiki*, Musashi sought refuge in the wake of the ambush (see Musashi's Duels). All are situated a few minutes by foot from Sagarimatsu, two of them laying abandoned in Musashi's time. One is the Kitayama Betsu-*in* monastery. Sitting atop a long flight of stairs, it is believed to have been founded in the early Kamakura period (1185–1333) and is closely associated with the Jōdo Shinshū monk Shinran (1173–1263), who visited the temple when he descended from Mount Hiei at the age of twenty-nine following a twenty-year period of pious meditation.

 The other alternative is the Konpuku temple. This temple dates all the way back to the early Heian period (794–1185), when it was founded in response to the dying wish of the Tendai monk Ennin (793–864). By Musashi's time, the temple had fallen into ruin, like the adjacent Kitayama Betsu-*in*. But during the late seventeenth century it was restored as a branch of the nearby Enkō temple, which itself dates back to 1667.

Hachidai Shrine

The *Bukōden* describes how, relating the run-up to his duel with Yoshioka Matashichirō to one of his *deshi*, Musashi said:

路に八幡の社前を経、憶、「我幸に不圖して神前に來れり。當祈勝利」と、及詣社壇、恭て鰐口の紐を執て將に打鳴さんとす。忽ち思ふ、「我常に佛神をも不信仰、而今此難を憚て頻に敬祷す。神其受や、諸吁怯矣」。即ち其紐を措て、孜々として下壇、慙愧ぢ汗流れて踵に至る。

On my way there I passed in front of the Hachiman shrine, and I thought to myself, "What good fortune that I should come before the gods by accident. I should take this opportunity and pray for victory." However, when I went up to the shrine's altar and took the crimson cord to sound the temple gong it suddenly occurred to me that normally I have never put any faith in gods and Buddhas. Yet, now, as I am facing imminent danger, I am suddenly eager to pay my respects. Ah, I must be flinching from danger. At that moment I let loose the gong's cord and stepped down from the altar. I was so deeply ashamed that I felt the sweat running down my back.

There is no shrine with the name Hachiman anywhere near Ichijōji, which is why it is now widely believed that the shrine Musashi visited on his way to his duel was the Hachidai shrine. This shrine, after all, is situated only a hundred yards east of Ichijōji. Asuming musashi stayed on some inn east of the capital, he must indeed have passed the grounds of the Hachidai shrine on his way to his duel.

Musashi's duel with the Yoshioka brothers is still celebrated at the **Hachidai shrine**, which is situated in a wooded area behind the Shisen monastery. Founded in 1294, the shrine owned large tracts of land, or *keidai*, in the surrounding area, including a place called Sagarimatsu. A huge trunk of pinewood, belonging to a tree that once graced the place of the duel is now kept on the shrine's precinct and venerated. In front of it stands a bronze statue of Musashi wielding two swords.

Edo Castle

It was during the first decade of the seventeenth century, while he was living and teaching in Edo, that, through the offices of his friend Mizuno Katsunari, Musashi was invited by Shōgun Tokugawa Ieyasu and his son, Hidetada, to give a demonstration of his art of swordsmanship at Edo castle. According to the *Bushū denraiki*:

武州兵法、將軍家達上聞、可被召出御沙汰ありといへ共、柳生但馬守殿、御師範として常住御前に侍席せらる。武州、柳生が下に立ん事を忌て、「若年より仕官の望なく、髪剃ず、爪とらず、法外の有様也。御免を奉蒙度」旨達て御斷申上らる。

The shōgunal house had taken notice of Musashi's art of heihō and word was sent to Musashi that they wanted to invite him.

Lord Yagyū Tajima no Kami Munenori, however, was already serv-
ing the Bakufu as shōgunal shihan. Musashi railed at the thought
of being placed below the Yagyū saying, "From my youth I have
held no ambitions for high office, and with my hair and nails uncut
I would cut a strange figure, so please forgive me for declining."

The same record describes how:

武州が繪を御覧被成度由にて、御屏風の繪に被仰付
。武蔵野に月の出たる所を、御屏風一杯に書て差上
げられしといえり。

In the end, the shōgun, having seen one of Musashi's paintings,
commissioned him to paint a folding screen. This time Musashi
obliged and presented to the shōgun a folding screen with a
scene of a rising moon over the plains of Musashi.

Moji Castle

It was following his departure from Edo that, in 1612, Musashi
visited Moji castle, on the northern tip of the southern island
of Kyushu, some ten miles northwest of the port of Kokura.
Its lord was Numata Nobumoto. It is not clear how he and
Musashi met. What is certain that Musashi was Nobumoto's
guest. The *Numata kaki*, the family records of the Numata
clan, compiled in 1672 by on of Nobumoto's descendants,
describes how:

延元樣門司に被成御座候時　或年宮本武蔵玄信豊前
へ罷越　二刀兵法の師を仕候。

One year, at the time when master Nobumoto resided at Moji
castle, Miyamoto Musashi Genshin visited Buzen and instructed
his lordship in the Nitō school of swordsmanship.

Moji castle, incidentally, was also the place where Musashi
sought refuge when, in the wake of his famed duel with
Sasaki Kojirō, he was being hunted down by the latter's *deshi*,
who were bent on revenge for their master's death.

Though **Moji castle** was dismantled in 1892 to make room for a gun placement of the Imperial Japanese Army in response to the increasing presence of foreign ships, a stone pillar still marks the place from where it guarded the Straits of Shimonoseki.

Ganryū Island

Ganryū island, or the island of the Gan school of swordsmanship (巌流島), is known for Musashi's famous duel with Sasaki Kojirō. Though not mentioned once in his own writings, the duel at the island of Ganryū is the most famous episode in Miyamoto Musashi's life and has come to epitomize his ingenious fencing skills.

Situated in the Shimonoseki straits, the narrow waters between the main island of Honshu and the southern island of Kyushu, the island was historically called **Funa**-*shima* (Boat Island) because of its boat-like shape. Up until the end of the Meiji period, the island was only a third of its present size. It was connected by a narrow riff of sand with the main island of Hikoshima. During the Taishō era, however, part of the shallow waters behind the riff was filled up with land, and the riff was severed from Hikoshima island, creating the much larger outline of the present island, now more commonly known as Ganryū Island.

Given Musashi's popularity, the island is now more widely known as Ganryū-*jima*, or Ganryū Island, but according to the *Kōkai fūhansō*:

この島の名は剣術使いの名によって名付けたという
のは誤りである。これは流儀の名前である。この流
儀を始めたのは上田宗入というものということであ
る。この者は、不見の磯に一年間結跏趺坐して波が

打つのを観じて兵法の工夫をして巌流と名付けた一
流を創始した。

The belief that this island was named after a swordsman by that name is a mistake, for it was named after a school of swordsmanship. The founder of this school was a man by the name of Ueda Sōnyū. He spent a year in meditation on a rocky beach and, observing how the waves broke on the rocks below, devised a school of swordsmanship that carries the name Garyū, or the "school of the rocks."

It is now widely believed that Musashi's opponent in this duel was a man by the name of Sasaki Kojirō, who happened to be a practitioner of the Ganryū school of swordsmanship. Though little is known about him, Kojirō is believed to have been a native of Echizen Province, and born in the town of Fukui toward the middle of the sixteenth century. At a young age, he entered the service of the powerful Asakura clan, which had its headquarters at Ichijōdani castle.

Hōzō Monastery

It was on one of his *musha shugyō* that Musashi visited Nara and stayed at the Hōzō-in, the monastery associated with the legendary master of *sōjutsu*, the art of fighting with the *yari*, **Hōzōin Kakuzenbō In'ei**. In'ei was a descendant of the Nakanomikado, a line of *sōhei* associated with Nara's Kōfuku temple. Drawing on their traditions, In'ei had founded his own school, the Hōzōin-*ryū*.

In'ei was also known for his mastery in the art of swordsmanship, an art he had first acquired under the tutelage of Toda Yosaemon, an exponent of Nenami Okuyama Jion's Nen-*ryū*, believed to be the oldest school of swordsmanship in Japan. It is said that, in total, In'ei had studied under as many as forty different masters of various weapons, chief among them the *yari*, the *naginata*, and the *tachi*. In'ei had long been the chief abbot of Nara's Hōzō monastery, but he retired from his duties to dedicate his last few years to the perfection of his art.

In'ei, at the time he and Musashi met, had just turned eighty-four. Unable to engage in combat with Musashi himself, he pitted Musashi against one of his senior pupils, the talented Okuzōin. The *Nitenki* describes how that same evening Musashi and Okuzōin met in the grounds of the **Hōzō monastery** to test each other's strength in a friendly bout (see Musashi's Bouts):

試合は、奥蔵院が得意の槍をもって構えたのに対し、武蔵は短い木剣一本のみでこれに対峙。奥蔵院が切っ先鋭く攻めかかったものの、武蔵は次々とその槍先をおさえ、ついには何の技もほどこさせないまま、相手に敗北を認めさせるのでした。武蔵の技量に感服した奥蔵院は、武蔵を泊めてもてなし、武術談議に花を咲かせて一夜を明かしたといいます。

The monk was armed with his yari. Musashi had chosen a short bokutō. They fought two bouts, but in neither was the monk able to gain the upper hand. At length, he bowed, expressed his deep admiration for Musashi's art of fencing, and asked him to stay at the Hōzō monastery, where he personally entertained him. They talked about the martial arts until dawn, when, at the sign of first light Musashi again departed.

Komatsuyama

Though Musashi might have participated both in Ieyasu's winter and summer campaign against Toyotomi Hideyori's forces ensconced at Osaka castle, there is only direct evidence of his involvement in the summer campaign. There is now little doubt that throughout that campaign Musashi was part of the escort of Mizuno Katsunari's son (see Musashi's Battles).

Katsunari, who had been put in command of a Tokugawa force of close to four thousand men, advanced on Osaka from Nara along the Nagao Kaidō, the old high road from the Nagao shrine in Katsuragi city to the ancient port of Sakai. At four o'clock in the afternoon of 1 June 1615, Katsunari's troops pitched camp at Kokubu, a hamlet on the southern bank of the Yamato River. Consisting of a few farms Kokubu marked a narrow pass between the river and a hill by the name of Komatsu. Immediately behind the hill, the river was joined by the Ishi River from the south. At dawn three more contingents reached Kokubu, causing Katsunari's force to swell to well over twenty thousand men.

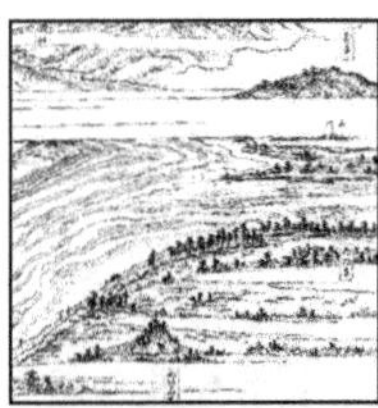

Only a few miles downstream, at the village of **Dōmyōji**, an equally large enemy force under the overall command of Gotō Mototsugu had gathered. His plan was to surprise Katsunari's forces before they crossed the pass that night. Breaking up camp at midnight amidst dense fog Mototsugu arrived on the opposite side of the Ishi River a few hours later, only to find that his allies had lost their way in the fog. His scouts, meanwhile, informed him Katsunari had already arrived and pitched camp at Kokubu. Intent on keeping the initiative, he ordered his three thousand men to ford the river and take up positions on Komatsu hill.

* *The village of Dōmyōji is named after a monastery belonging to the Shingon sect founded by the ancestors of Sugawara no Muchizane (Tenman Daijizai Tenjin). The nearby Dōmyōji Tenmangu shrine is dedicated to the great Heian court official.*

Katsunari's scouts, too, had spotted their enemy's movement. By the time Mototsugu and his men had negotiated the hill, Katsunari's warriors, led by Okuda Tadatsugu, were ascending the hill's eastern slopes, pushing Mototsugu back towards the hill's shallow summit. Greatly outnumbered he managed to keep his position, hoping all the time his allies would come to his rescue. They failed to arrive, and when at ten o'clock Mototsugu was hit by a bullet he committed ritual suicide, but not before he had ordered his *kaishaku* to burry his head in the mud so that it could not be collected by Katsunari's men and presented to Ieyasu.

* *A* kaishaku *was the person, usually a trusted friend, whose role it was to behead the one committing* seppuku *and thus relieve him from the terrible pain that accompanied this ritual.*

His troops began to descend the hill toward the Ishi river in disarray. But Katsunari, together with his son Katsutoshi and his mounted escort including Musashi, had meanwhile rounded **Komatsu hill** through the pass, thereby executing a pincer movement he had proposed during a war council the day before.

Today, Komatsuyama seems a small island amid the urban sprawl of Fujii's outskirts. It still overlooks the Ishi River, whose course has been constrained by steep concrete embankments. Climbing a narrow flight of steps on the hill's western side one can reach the summit of the hill. There, the fierce fighting that it witnessed is still commemorated by the grave of Okuda Tadatsugu, the general who led his men up the hill's eastern flank to face Mototsugu's forces.

Dōmyōji

The clash at Dōmyōji came directly in the wake of Gotō Mototsugu's death. Having routed Mototsugu's troops on Komatsu hill, Katsunari and his fellow commanders pursued the Toyotomi troops across the Ishi River toward the small village of Dōmyōji. Informed of Mototsugu's death, another Toyotomi general, Susuki Kanesuke, had taken command of the fleeing troops, regrouped them, and launched a counter-attack to drive Katsunari's forces back into the Ishi River.

It is this juncture in the battle, in the early afternoon of 2 June 1615, that is described in vivid detail by Mizuno Katsunari's diary, when it relates how the Tokugawa general, his son, and a mounted escort including Musashi, arrived at a small stone bridge set amid rice paddies:

先に拙者（勝成）二番に中山勘解由、三番に水野美作守、四番目に村瀬左馬、それを乗り越すと、本多左京の軍勢が追い崩され、その橋の際まで逃げかかってきたので、右四人の者、馬より降り槍を取って突き掛かり、敵を退け、藤井寺まで進撃した。

I was the first to mount the bridge, followed by Nakayama Kageyu, Mizuno Katsutoshi, and Murase Saba. Passing the bridge, we found that the forces of Honda Sakyō had been pushed back and had fled into the paddies flanking the bridge, upon which we dismounted from our horses. And taking our lances, we pursued the enemy all the way back to Fujiidera.

The *Kōkō zatsuroku* describes how Musashi was "standing on a bridge, brandishing his long *bokutō*, and being cheered on, he cast the enemy troops off the bridge left and right."

One of the forces who had descended on Dōmyōji under Motsugu's command was that of **Sanada Yukimura**. Given the dense mist on the morning of the attack, he, like the other Toyotomi generals, had failed to join with Mototsugu's forces, thereby contributing to the latter's routing at Komatsu hill. Instead, they had reached the village of Konda, on the southern side of the ancient burial mound of Emperor Ōjin (200–310). It was there that they were joined by the Kanesuke's remaining men after they had been routed a second time by Katunari's men.

Intriguingly, on the south side of the burial mound (*kofun*) is still an ancient stone bridge. Called a *taikobashi*, or *taiko* bridge, after the shape of the Japanese *taiko* drum, the bridge is situated on the grounds of the Konda Hachiman-gū. The main hall of this shrine was built on the request of Emperor Kinmei (539–571), making it the oldest shrine celebrating Hachiman, the god of war. The small stone bridge is called the **Hōjō bridge**. On the 15th of September, during the annual Autumn Festival, a *mikoshi*, or portable shrine, used to be carried across the bridge and to the crest of Emperor Ōjin's burial mound.

* *The area around Fujiidera is known for its many keyhole-shaped* kofun, *ancient imperial burial mounds dating back to the aptly named Kofun period (250–538).*

The bridge is featured in old drawings of the area and probably dates back to Musashi's time. Yet, it is probably not the bridge mentioned in the *Kōkō zatsuroku*. For that it is simply too small. If it was on the grounds of the Konda Hachiman-gū, the author would not have forgotten where it was (see Musashi's Battles). More importantly, the bridge is not situated along the main route through Dōmyōji at the time. Katsunari and his men were marching on Osaka along the Nagao Kaidō. The stone bridge mentioned in the records, therefore, was probably situated somewhere along the high road just north of the Dōmyō Tenmangu shrine, not more than a few hundred meters from the ford across the Ishi River.

Osaka Castle

The next day, 3 June, the fighting around Osaka castle continued relentless and unforgiving. Trying to keep the initiative, the western forces sought to crush Ieyasu's troops at Tennōji, on the doorstep of the ancient Shitennō temple, a few miles south of Osaka castle. Executed as a hammer-and-anvil operation, the frontal attack was led by Sanada Yukimura, while the rear flank was led by the indomitable Akashi Takenori. For some time the odds hung in the balance, but finally, at three o'clock in the afternoon, at the cost of huge casualties, Ieyasu drove them back into the castle.

A scramble now ensued among the eastern troops to be the first to mount the walls of the painfully exposed castle. Musashi, still part of Katsutoshi's escort, was one of the first to enter the Sakura Mon, the main southern gate to the castle, north of which water still filled the castle's moats. And he was with Katsutoshi and his father when they planted the Mizuno banner over the imposing entrance.

Himeji Castle

In the summer of 1617, Musashi was the guest of Honda Tadamasa, the new lord of **Himeji castle**. Both had taken part in the siege of Osaka castle, and on the swordsman's request, he made Musashi's adopted son, Mikinosuke a page to his eldest son, Tadatoki.

Not everyone in Himeji was as hospitable as Tadamasa. Some of the senior Honda retainers were unhappy with Musashi's presence. They were outraged by the blatant effrontery with which Musashi was promoting his Enmei school of swordsmanship. Not long after he had met with Honda Tadamasa, he had opened a *dōjō* in Himeji where he built up a large following of devoted students from all over the region.

Most offensive to Tadamasa's newly arrived retainers was a large signboard Musashi had erected in front of his *dōjō* that read: Musashi, Japan's Foremost Master of Swordsmanship." The majority of Tadamasa's men were practitioners of the Tōgun-*ryū*, a school of swordsmanship that had its origin in the Toda-*ryū*, which in turn went back to the ancient Chūjō-*ryū*. Founded by the great Kawasaki Kaginosuke, the Tōgun school of swordsmanship was considered by many to be the official fencing style of the house of Honda. Whenever they passed his *dōjō* on some errand, they returned to their quarters with more exasperated tales of the eccentric braggart with his odd style of dressing, his long hair, and his unusual style of fighting with two swords.

Word of the unrest among his retainers came to Tadamasa's ears and before long he felt compelled to act. The *Bisan hōkan* describes how:

本多忠政は、これを聞いて、「宮本が真に日本一の
達人ならば、我が家臣にしよう。もしそうでなけれ
ば、試合して恥辱を与えて放逐するがよい」という
。そこで、姫路藩士第一の剣客、三宅軍太夫を遣わ
して、武蔵の武芸を試験させることになった。

When Honda Tadamasa heard of the unrest he said, "If Musashi really is the greatest swordsman in the realm, I would want to make him one of my retainers. If he is not, the shame of defeat in duel will surely make him leave on his own accord." At this, he summoned Himeji's chief swordsman, Miyake Gundayū, and instructed him to put Musashi's martial skills to the test.

Akashi Castle

Sometime during the 1620s, Musashi became the guest of Ogasawara Tadazane (1596–1667). Like Musashi, Tadazane had participated in the Osaka campaigns, and in reward for his service he had been awarded the fiefdom of Akashi in Musashi's ancestral province of Harima. It is not clear when the two met, but it was probably not long afterward that Musashi became Tadazane's guest.

To guard his newly won fiefdom and to boost its economy

Tadazane began the construction of **Akashi castle**, a castle town, as well as a harbor. With his experience of siege warfare, Musashi served as an adviser to the *zōei bugyō*, the construction magistrate in charge of the whole project. Recognizing the warrior's artistic qualities Tadazane also put Musashi in charge of the design of the castle gardens, as well as a small tea house. The *Seiryūwa* describes how:

三の丸の西の端に南北に細長い捨曲輪があって、芝原であった所に、忠政は新しく樹木屋敷という遊興所を造るため作庭を宮本武蔵に命じ。

Facing the western side of the third bailey of Akashi castle was a narrow strip of enclosed land stretching northward. On the part that was barren and uninhabited, the lord ordered Musashi to build a yashiki surrounded by trees and shrubs.

For more than a decade Musashi remained in Akashi. But his life was uprooted once more when Tadazane was promoted to the Kokura fiefdom on the southern island of Kyushu, and Musashi's son, Iori, who had meanwhile entered Tadazane's service, moved down with him.

Sadly, today, the gardens originally designed by Musashi lie once again barren. In 1922, during a major redesign of the castle gardens, many of the trees, shrubs, and rocks were transferred to create a new garden in the vicinity of the **Otome pond**, on the castle's southeastern side. After the war, the original gardens were turned into an athletic field and have remained so until the present day. In 2003, to attract more visitors to Akashi castle on the wave of a Musashi boom, the gardens around Otome pond were renamed Musashi Teien, or the Musashi Gardens.

Kasadera Kannon

During one of his visits to Nagoya Musashi is believed to

have stayed at the Tōkōin, one of the twelve lodgings for priests of the Ryūfukuji, an old temple in the town's southern quarters that dated back to the eighth century.

Better known as the **Kasadera Kannon,** the temple was founded in 733 by a monk named Zenkō when he carved an image of the Jūichimen Kannon, the bodhisattva with eleven faces, from a piece of driftwood from the nearby Tenpaku river.

According to one anecdote, the temple was visited toward the end of the 9th century by Fujiwara Kanehira (875–935), a man whom Musashi would have considered his distant ancestor. A Heian court official and a renowned player of the *biwa*, he had come to pay homage to the Jūichimen Kannon. The rainy season had started and it was pelting down when to his dismay he found that the roof of the building in which the relic was housed had long since collapsed.

It was only when Kanehira entered the dilapidated structure that he spotted a young woman, holding up an umbrella to protect the withered *kannon* from the raging elements. Touched to his poetic core, he took her with him to the capital, gave her the name Ōshōhime, and married her. From then on, the temple was popularly known as the Kasadera (笠寺), the Umbrella Temple.

While staying at the Tōkōin, Musashi was invited by Tokugawa Yoshinao (1601–50), the *daimyō* of Owari (the fief of which Nagoya castle was the headquarters) to give a demonstration of his art of swordsmanship in a duel in Yoshinao's presence. The *Mukashibanashi* describes how:

相手すつと立合うと、武蔵、組たる二刀のまま、大の切っ先を相手の鼻の先へつけて、一間の内を一遍回し歩きて、勝負かくの如くに御座候と、申し上げし。

When his opponent suddenly opened the attack, Musashi crossed his two swords, training the tip of his long sword on the tip of his adversary's nose, thus steadily forcing the latter backward until they had traced the circumference of the whole dōjō, and said "this is the way in which I fight duels."

One of the artifacts still kept by the temple today is a *bokutō* crafted by Musashi during his stay at the temple. More important is a calligraphy from Musashi's hand. Drawn by the swordsman as a token of gratitude to the temple's abbot, it carries the words Namu Tenman Daijizai Tenjin (南無天満大自在天神), an old text expressing reverence to another great Heian court official, Sugawara no Muchizane (Tenman Daijizai Tenjin). Michizane was a famed poet-scholar, whose life had taken a tragic turning when he was unjustly exiled to Kyushu.

Today one can still visit a memorial stone in the temple's cemetery commemorating Musashi's death. It was erected in 1744 by Sōda Hōsei, the fifth-generation practitioner of Musashi's Enmei-*ryū* in Owari.

Fukuyama Castle

During the Kan'ei era (1624–29) Musashi visited Mizuno Katsunari (1564–1651) at his headquarters of Fukuyama castle. He stayed at the *yashiki* of Nakayama Shigemori, one of Mizunari's chief retainers, who held a banquet in honor of his guest.

Musashi's visit to Fukuyama is immortalized in a large stone that had become the swordsman's favorite place to sit

while sojourning in his host's garden. Though Shigemori's *yashiki* has long since been destroyed, the stone on which Musashi used to sit has been moved to the precincts of the Bingo Go-kuni shrine, situated on the castle ground's northern perimeter, where it graces the temple grounds under the name of Musashi **Meisō Ishi** (Musashi's Meditative Stone).

It is not clear how exactly Katsunari and Musashi first met. The first document to suggest a relationship—if not outright friendship—between Musashi and Katsunari is a recently discovered copy of Musashi's *Heidō kagami* addressed to none other than Katsunari himself. The document is dated "an auspicious day," in the twelfth month of the thirteenth year of Keichō (January 1609). This means that Musashi had already met and befriended Katsunari by the time he was only twenty-five when he was still living in Edo developing and promoting his Enmei school of swordsmanship.

What is certain is that Musashi served under Katsunari during the summer siege of Osaka castle. Musashi was the fourth among a group of ten mounted warriors attached to none other than Sakushū-*sama*, the honorary name of Katsunari's son, Katsutoshi. It is quite possible that Musashi's immediate commander in that battle was Nakayama Shigemori. That would explain why the roll call (*Osaka o-jin no otomo*) on which Musashi's name appears was rediscovered in 1984 among the possessions of a certain Nakayama Fumio (Nagoya), a direct descendant of Nakayama Shigemori (Shōgen), who was one of Katsunari's chief retainers.

In reward for his contribution to Ieyasu's Osaka campaigns, Mitsunari was initially promoted to the Kōriyama-*han*, a fief of sixty thousand *koku* in Yamato Province. Given Katsunari's huge contribution, the promotion was already frowned upon by his contemporaries, not least by himself, as he had expected a fief of at least two-hundred thousand *koku*. Yet it had been his reckless valor, which had vexed Ieyasu (who could ill afford to lose such a valuable ally), that had cost Katsunari a more lofty promotion.

Katsunari's pride was somewhat restored in 1619, when Ieyasu's son, Hidetada, promoted him to the Fukuyama fief in the province of Bingo. At the time, the fief was still only worth a hundred-thousand *koku* (another one thousand were added in 1626), but it did control the western part of the Inland Sea, making it—as well as Katsunari's appointment—of strategic importance to the Bakufu. In 1622, to better police the sea, he therefore abandoned his more inland headquarters of Kannabe castle, for the newly built Fukuyama castle at the mouth of the Ashida River.

Nagoya Castle

Some of Musashi's friendly bouts were the result of an invitation by a feudal lord to demonstrate his art of swordsmanship. One of the most high-ranking men to attend such a demonstration was Tokugawa Yoshinao (1601–50), the *daimyō* of Owari and lord of **Nagoya castle**. The ninth son of Tokugawa Ieyasu, Yoshinao had been only fourteen years old when he took part in the siege of Osaka castle, attending his father's camp during the winter campaign and leading reinforcements during the Battle of Tennōji (1615).

From a young age, Yoshinao had taken a profound interest in the martial arts. Like his father, Ieyasu (who had invited Musashi to Edo castle for a demonstration), he patronized the Yagyū Shinkage school of swordsmanship. His chief fencing instructor was Yagyū Toshiyoshi, nephew of the famed Yagyū Munenori. In his youth, Yoshinao had submitted himself to five years of intensive practice under Toshiyoshi's guidance and had grown into a highly accomplished swordsman.

The *Mukashibanashi* describes how, sometime during the fall of 1632:

宮本武蔵がなごやへ来りしを召され、於御前兵法つかひ仕合せし時、相手すつと立合と、武蔵くみたる二刀のま丶、大の切先を相手の鼻のさきへつけて、一間のうちを一ぺんまわしあるきて、勝負如此二御座候と申上し。

Miyamoto Musashi was invited to Nagoya to demonstrate his art of swordsmanship in his lordship's presence, when his opponent suddenly opened the attack. But Musashi crossed his two swords, trained the tip of his long sword on his adversary's nose, and steadily forced him back until they had traced the circumference of the whole dōjō, and said "this is the way in which I fight duels."

Matsuyama Castle

It was in the spring of 1633, that Musashi visited **Iyo Matsuyama castle** and was the guest of Matsudaira Katsutaka. Only five years younger than Musashi, Katsutaka was known for his great love of swordsmanship. He was the son of one of Ieyasu's most senior vassals and had held a string of important positions within the Bakufu. That same spring, he had moved down to the province of Iyo, on the island of Shikoku, to take up temporary residence on the grounds of Matsuyama castle. The former lord of Matsuyama castle had passed away and the Bakufu decided that henceforth the Matsuyama domain was to be governed by a member of the Matsudaira, the clan from which the Tokugawa descended. It was Katsutaka's duty to prepare the *hikiwatashi*, the castle's smooth transfer from one clan to another.

Matsutaka did not live at Matsuyama castle. The *Bushū denraiki* describes how, rather than staying at the castle:

寛永比、武州、松平出雲守殿の家にあり。雲州の家頼に多力の兵法者あり。出雲、彼と武蔵との勝負を望まる。

In the era of Kan'ei [1624–44], Musashi stayed at the mansion of Lord Matsudaira Katsutaka. Among the retainers of Lord Katsutaka there were a great number of heihōsha, and his lordship wished to see them match themselves against Musashi.

Following the contest, Musashi remained at Matsutaka's mansion in Matsuyama for more than half a year until, in the fall of 1634, he traveled down along the Inland Sea toward Kokura to join his son Iori, who was in the service of Ogasawara Tadazane, the new lord of Kokura castle.

Kokura Castle

Later in life, when Iori had moved to Kokura with his master, Ogasawara Tadazane, Musashi also temporarily came to live with his son on the castle grounds of **Kokura castle**. And it was during this period, according to the *Bushū denraiki*, he had his well-known bout with Takagi Umanosuke Shigesada:

武州、大太刀を逆手に持、右馬允が打所を入込て、面を強くひしぐ。ひしがれて身のゝる所を、身をかけて、大指を以て胸をばぐつと突て、あをのけに突倒す。右馬允恐怖し、見物の面々肝膽を作る。

Holding his large tachi in a backhand grip Musashi stooped and struck Umanosuke in the face as he lunged toward him. Umanosuke was thrown back by the impact, but before he knew it Musashi was upon him, thrusting his thumb in Umanosuke's solar plexus and causing him to fall over backward. Umanosuke was terrified and the onlookers were dumbfounded.

Kokura castle was also the place where Musashi experienced

one of the most painful events in his life: the loss of his one-and-only natural child. Tachibana Minehira, alias Tanji Hōkin, is the only one to recount this episode in Musashi's life in his *Bushū denraiki*:

武州は、悲嘆限りなく、朝から夕方まで小児の死骸を膝に置いて、嘆き暮らされた。さまざまに申し上げ慰めても、一向に聞き受けられない。武州には不似合な行いだと、隨仕の面々もいう,,,その後、死骸を葬ったのかとも問われなかった。生涯、その女児の話をされることはなかったという。

Musashi was inconsolable with grief and wept from dawn till dusk while he cradled the remains of the infant in his lap. People tried to console him but he did not hear them. Even his followers said that this was unbecoming in their master...I did not even hear whether he buried the remains, for throughout his life Musashi never again talked about the baby girl.

Hara Castle

It was while living in Kokura with his son, Iori, that Musashi became part of the campaign to suppress the Shimabara Rebellion. It would be the last time Musashi saw action on the battlefield. The rebellion was centered around **Hara castle**, an abandoned castle on the Shimabara Peninsula in western Kyushu.

The Shimabara Rebellion was also the first—and only—time Musashi was joined by his son, Iori (see Musashi's Children). Not a warrior like his father, Iori probably served Ogasawara Tadazane in a civil capacity, safely behind the battle lines. Yet it seems Iori was of great use, for the *Harima kagami* claims that he "rendered distinguished services to his lordship" in the course of the battle, in reward for which his stipend was increased to three thousand *koku*, until he was finally raised to the rank of senior retainer.

This important appointment had come about partly through the generous mediation of Arima Naozumi. The lord of Nobeoka castle in the province of Hyūga, he originally hailed from Hizen, and Hara castle stood on his former domains. Due to his intimate knowledge of the terrain he had played a leading role in the castle's siege, in the course of which he had come to know Iori intimately.

Writing to Naozumi in the wake of the battle, Musashi expressed his gratitude:

被思召付尊礼忝次第二奉存候。随而せがれ伊織儀、御耳二立申通大慶奉存候。拙者儀、老足可被御推量候。貴公様御意之様、御家中衆へも手先二而申かわし候。殊御父子共本丸迄早々被成御座候通驚目申候。

that my son Iori was entrusted with the role of evaluating our military actions following the battle. I also believe that I conducted your men to the positions you had in mind, and everyone was full of praise about the swiftness with which you and your father managed to press on to the castle's inner circle.

Uniquely, he also gave a glimpse of how he himself had fared during the siege:

拙者も石二あたりすねたちかね申故、御目見得二も祇候不仕候。

As for myself, I was struck on the shins twice by rocks, making it impossible for me to put any weight on my legs at present, so I beg your pardon for not coming down to thank you in person.

The siege of Hara castle was to be the last time the Tokugawa hegemony was seriously disturbed and the last time Musashi saw action. He was now fifty-four years old and had taken part in as many as six battles, all of them on Kyushu soil except, of course, the Osaka campaign. His first experience of the battlefield had been more than forty years earlier, on the island's northern shore, when during the fierce battle on the plains of Ishigaki he first saw action under Kuroda Yoshitaka. In the subsequent siege of Tomiku castle he had brazenly climbed its defenses, wrestling with a lance thrust through a loophole by one of its occupants. Now he had done his utmost to keep Lord Nagatsugu from indulging in similar antics, incurring serious wounds himself as a result—he was beginning to feel old and weary of the battlefield.

Kumamoto Castle

In 1640, having looked around for a place to spend his last days, Musashi accepted the invitation of Hosokawa Tadatoshi (1586–1641), the *daimyō* of the Kumamoto fief in southern Kyushu. The *Bukōden* describes how:

忠利公より月俸十七口現米三百石を賜ぶ。蓋し遊客たるを以て、諸士の列に不配。居宅は熊本千葉城の高き所也り。

Lord Tadatoshi granted Musashi a stipend sufficient to support seventeen servants, and also gave him three hundred koku in kind. Perhaps it was because Musashi stayed in his lordship's domain as a guest that he was not taken up in his retinue of retainers. His dwelling was situated at the high place of Kumamoto's Chiba castle.

Having been written by Toyoda Masanaga, a retainer of the Nagaoka, who in turn were close vassals to the Hosokawa, it is not surprising that the *Bukōden* is one of the few records to mention where exactly Musashi lived after he had settled in Kumamoto. Somewhat confusingly, the place Masanaga describes as Chiba castle was situated within the walls of **Kumamoto castle**. Situated inside one of the curves of the Tsubai River, on the northeastern side of the castle grounds, Chiba castle was in fact also the original site of Kumamoto castle.

Chiba castle had once been the residence of the Ideta, an old clan from Kyushu. It was erected in the second half of the fifteenth century by Ideta Hidenobu, but later replaced by Kumamoto castle, albeit at a slightly different location. Today, the area is still known as the Chiba castle township, or Chibajō-*machi*, although it is now situated outside the castle grounds. The old castle well, believed by many to have once been used by Musashi, is still there.

It seems that, from the moment Musashi began on his life's work, his seminal *Gorin no sho*, the aging swordsman spent less and less time at his *yashiki* on the former grounds of Chiba castle and more and more time in the Reigan Cave—so much so, that, again according to the *Bukōden*:

世上何かと奇怪の浮説あり。寄之公、放鷹に詫して岩戸に至り、武公を諫て、再び千葉城の旧宅に歸らしむ。

Strange but groundless rumors were beginning to circulate among the populace and, feigning that he had gone out to hunt with falcons, Lord Nagaoka Yoriyuki prevailed on Musashi to return to the old residence of Chiba castle.

It was at his *yashiki* on the former grounds of Chiba castle, too, that, on 13 June 1645, Musashi passed away peacefully at the age of sixty.

Reigan Cave

The most fascinating and at the same time intriguing site connected to Musashi is undoubtedly the Reigan Cave, or Reigan-*dō* (霊嚴洞) in Japanese. The cave, situated on Mount Iwato is the cave Musashi visited frequently during his last years in the castle town of Kumamoto to write his magnum opus, the *Gorin no sho*, the *Book of Five Rings*. The name Reigan is comprised of the two characters of *rei* (霊), or spirit, and *gan*, (嚴), or great rock, which is also the first character of Ganryū Island, the island on which Musashi fought his celebrated duel with Sasaki Kojirō.

Mount Iwato is situated just west of Kumamoto castle. Musashi, at this time, was living on the grounds of Kumamoto castle, where, with the blessing of Hosokawa Tadatoshi, he had settled to spend his last days. Two years earlier, Hosokawa Tadatoshi had passed away and it is believed that it was on the request of his son, Hosokawa Mitsunao (1619–50), that Musashi visited the cave in the mountain to record the secrets of his school of swordsmanship.

The **Reigan Cave** was already a place of pilgrimage in Musashi's days, for the cave is situated on the grounds of the Unganzenji, a temple belonging to the Sōtō sect. The temple is said to have been founded during the Northern and Southern Courts period (1334–1392) by the Chinese monk Dōng Líng Yong Yú (Tōryō Eiyo, in Japanese), who visited Japan on the invitation of Ashikaga (1306–1352).

At the rear wall of the cave, thoroughly hidden from view behind two **latticed screens**, is a stone image of the Kannon Bosatsu (Avalokitesvara), the Bodhisattva of Compassion. She is the temple's principal object of worship, by virtue of which the Reigan Cave is essentially its inner sanctum, or *oku no in*.

The Reigan Cave is believed to have been visited by the Heian poetess Higaki. Once a courtesan at the Heian court known for her wanton sensuality, Higaki fell on hard times following a riot in which her house was looted and burned. She took up living in an old shack along the Shira River, where she was visited by the then governor, Fujiwara no Okinori.

Asked to bring him some water, she composed a poem in which she lamented the course her life had taken:

年ふれば
我が黒髪も
白河の
みづはくむまで
老いにけるかな

Since the years have passed
my black hair, too,
Like the white river
Shirakawa

Musashi does not mention the Reigan Cave in his own writings, but then again, he hardly mentions any of the places where he resided throughout his life. Yet it was here, amid the tranquility of the cave's interior, that the swordsman found the inspiration to write his seminal work. That much, at least, is borne out by the *Bushū denraiki* and the the *Bukō-den*. Thus the *Bushū denraiki* describes the moment Musashi first took up his brush:

寛永二十年、武州六十歳、肥の後州岩戸山に登り、觀世音菩薩を拜し、佛前に於て、天道と觀世音を鏡として、十月十日の寅の一天に筆を執て、兵書五巻を記せる。地水火風空と號す.

In the twentieth year of Kanei [1643], at the age of sixty, Musashi climbed Mount Iwato where he worshipped the Kannon Bosatsu. And on the tenth day of the tenth month [21 November], at the third sign of the zodiac, and in the light of the Kannon and the Heavenly Way, he took up his brush and recorded the five scrolls on the art of heihō. *He named them the scrolls of earth, water, fire, wind, and heaven.*

Though this would suggest that Musashi wrote his lengthy work in a single burst of inspiration, it is more likely that he did so over the course of several months, if not years. This seems to be borne out by the *Bukōden* which describes how, after more than a year, he still sought out the Reigan Cave, even though he was now on the brink of death:

正保二年之春、武公病なり。府中の紛囂を厭ひ、岩戸に至り、霊岩洞の裏に入り、静に終命の期了せんんとす。

In the summer of the second year of Shōhō [1645], Musashi fell ill. Finding the hustle and bustle of town disagreeable, he went up to Mount Iwato, where he entered the Reigan cave so that he might quietly await his end.

Today, the Reigan Cave has become the prime destination of Musashi aficionados around the world. The sense of mysticism is enhanced by a multitude of sitting statues that grace the flank of the mountain, which at the same time lend it a somewhat eery quality. Donated to the temple by a certain Fuchida Yagihei, a merchant from Kumamoto who lived during the early nineteenth century, they represent the *gohyaku rakan*, or the **Five Hundred Enlightened Followers of Buddha.**

In a small building next to the entrance called **Hōmotsu-***kan* (Treasure store), artifacts from the Hosokawa estate are on display behind a glass window. Among them are several mounted reproductions of Musashi's paintings, including a copy of his famous self-portrait, the original of which is kept at the Shimada Museum of Art in Kumamoto. Pride of place in this small exhibition is a large *bokutō* crafted from a traditional oar and, according to a small notice, the very weapon with which he defeated Sasaki Kojirō on the island of Funashima (see Musashi's Weapons).

Musashi's Grave

As if to illustrate the eagerness with which various groups seem to claim Musashi's heritage, even the place where the great swordsman is supposed to be buried is contested. Fact is that Musashi died in the vicinity of Kumamoto on 13 June 1645. However, it is not clear where exactly his remains were interred on his death, whether they were later moved, and where they are currently resting.

According to the *Bukōden* Musashi was initially buried in the village of Oe in Kumamoto's Akita district. Today, neither the village Oe nor the district of Akita any longer exist, as the village has been swallowed up by Kumamoto's suburbs, while the district of Akita was abolished as a result of land reforms during the Meiji era. In Musashi's day, however, the village of Oe (小江) was situated on the eastern banks of the **Shira River**, only a mile or so upstream from Kumamoto castle. Spelled with a different initial character, this part of Kumamoto is now called Ōe (大江).

According to the *Heihō senshi denki* Musashi's remains were (at some stage) recovered from the grave in Akita and transferred to Kokura "on the request of Ogasawara Tadazane, who thought it more fitting that Musashi be buried in Kokura, near the rest of his descendants." If Musashi's remains were indeed transferred to Kokura, it is more likely that this was done by his son, Iori, when, in 1654, on the tenth anniversary of his father's death, he erected a monument on the crest of **Temukeyama**, a small hill on the outskirts of Akazaka.

It might have been at that juncture that Iori had Musashi's tombstone in Kumamoto moved to a village called Yuge, on the opposite bank of the Shira River, some five miles

upstream from Kumamoto. Yuge was situated along the Ōzu Kaidō, the old high road that connected Kumamoto to the rest of Japan. Called Musashizuka, or the Musashi burial mound, it is today located in the Ryūta township in Kumamoto's Kita (northern) ward. Known as **Musashizuka Park** and graced with a life-size statue of the swordsman, the site is now widely recognized as Musashi's true gravesite and as such is visited by thousands of Musashi aficionados each year.

There is, however, yet another contender for the claim to be Musashi's burial site. This is what has come to be known as the Nishi no Musashizuka, or the western Musashi burial mound, as it is situated in Kumamoto's western Shimasaki ward. Engraved with the inscription *Shingen Koji*, or "Buddhist layman Shingen," a **withered rock** flanked by two lanterns marsk the place where some believe Musashi's remains rest until this day. It is, however, probably the grave of a descendant of one of Musashi's most trusted followers, Terao Motomenosuke Nobuyuki (1621–88), whose grave lies nearby. It was probably out of devotion for the founding father of their school of swordsmanship, that Nobuyuki's descendant also took on the name of Shingen (see Musashi's Deshi).

There is one more site erected in the wake of Musashi's death. Hidden away on the grounds of the former Taishō temple, it is situated next to the **grave of Akiyama Wanao**, and flanked by a narrow pole reading "*Miyamoto Musashi kyōyō-tō*" (tower for the repose of Musashi's spirit). In fact it is a traditional *gorintō* still widely used for memorial monuments and tombs.

Kokura Monument

The **Musashi Kokura Monument** was erected in 1654 on the initiative of Musashi's adopted son, Miyamoto Iori, nine years after Musashi had passed away. Inscribed on the fifteen feet high obelisk-like stone memorial is a lengthy epitaph celebrating the swordsman's life, his exploits, and his character. The monument stands on the crest of Temukeyama, a shallow hill on the outskirts of Akazaka, in the northern district of the port of Kokura that looks out over the beautiful Straits of Shimonoseki. Standing on the crest of the hill, one can just make out the island of Funashima in the distance, protruding from behind the main island of Hikoshima. At the time of its erection, the monument lay within Iori's fief in the district of Kikunokōri within the larger Kokura fiefdom in Buzen.

It is believed that Akiyama Wanao (1618–73), abbot of the Taishō temple in Kumamoto, composed the *Kokura hibun*. During Musashi's last years in Kumamoto, Wanao befriended the swordsman and, according to the *Bukōden*, helped him by proofreading his *Gorin no sho*. He gave the swordsman his posthumous name and gave him the last rites at his funeral service at the Taishō temple. In 1654, nine years after Musashi's death, Wanao composed the lengthy epitaph in response to a request by Musashi's son, Iori.

In 1887, the area underwent reconstruction to accommodate a battery guarding the Strait of Shimonoseki over which it looks. The monument was transferred to the nearby Enmeijiyama (Akazaka). Iori's grave found a new place at the southern foot of the Temukeyama, close to the entrance of what is now called Temukeyama park. Since then Musashi's monument has returned to its rightful place, at the top of Temukeyama, but the graves of Iori and his descendants remain at the foot of the hill, close to the entrance of what is now called Temukeyama park.

MUSASHI'S DUELS

In his *Gorin no sho* Musashi clearly states that from the age of twelve to the age of twenty-seven, he fought as many as sixty duels, but that he was never defeated. Sadly, he spends only a few words on the men he met in duel, and the chroniclers of his time recorded only a limited number of those fights. Indeed, those that did recount his deadly duels did so long after the swordsman had passed away, drawing from oral transmissions or records of those who knewn him alive.

Luckily, the records that have survived enable us to reconstruct some of the pivotal duels in the swordsman's life: his first duel, his encounters with the members of the Yoshioka clan, and the great showdown with Sasaki Kojirō on the island of Funashima. Taken together, they give us a unique insight into the enigmatic swordsman's approach to the art of combat, an art that relied on more than just his superior dexterity with the sword.

Arima Kihei

Musashi's duel with **Arima Kihei** is the first recorded duel of the young Musashi (who by western reckoning was only twelve years old) on a track along the Sayo River near his mother's hometown of Hirafuku. The little that is known about Kihei is recorded in the *Bushū denraiki*, which describes how:

十三歳の時、新当流の兵法者で有馬喜兵衛という者が、播州にやって来た。浜辺に矢来を結び、金磨きの高札を立てて、試合を望み次第いたす旨、それに書き記した。

When Bennosuke had reached the age of twelve a man named Arima Kihei, a warrior of the Shintō school of fencing, visited the province of Harima. He staked out a bamboo fence on a vacant plot of land and put up a gilded notice saying that he was keen for anyone who wanted to engage with him in a shiai.

Though little is known about the man with whom Musashi fought his first duel, the same record describes the duel and its gruesome outcome at great length. According to the *Bushū denraiki* (which still refers to Musashi by his infant name):

辨之助來たり、やらひの戸を押開き、「喜兵衛とは
其方か、さあ、試闘まいらん」と聲をかけ、走り掛
て杖を以て打しくる。喜兵衛も立揚り、抜打に切し
くる。然れ共、辨之助は走りかかり、喜兵衛は牀几
を立揚り切りしけし故、身近く、双方疵しかずして
、腕と腕げ肩にとどまる。辨之助、杖をすて、かひ
くぐりざま、肩にあげて、ましさかさまに落し、杖
をし取、つづけ打に十四五打、即時に打殺す。

Bennosuke pushed open the fence and called out "are you Kihei, well, let's duel," upon which he ran up to Kihei and struck him with his cane. Kihei now rose and drew his sword and struck out at the young boy. Yet, as Bennosuke had run up to him, and Kihei had struck the moment he had stood up from his camp stool, both were too close to inflict any wounds on the other and they remained locked in an embrace, their hands above each other's shoulders. Bennosuke now suddenly dropped his cane, ducked to the floor, put his shoulders under his opponent, and toppled him head first to the floor. Then he took up his cane again and killed Kihei with a succession of fourteen to fifteen blows.

Members of the Yoshioka Clan

When Musashi arrived in Kyoto to challenge the Yoshioka clan, the Yosh-ioka-*ryū* had been the official fencing school of the Ashikaga Bakufu for close to a century. It had been founded in the early sixteenth century by Yoshioka Naomoto, a senior retainer of *shōgun*

Ashikaga Yoshiharu. According to the *Yoshioka-den*, the family record of the Yoshioka clan:

元方季方之流西而、佐藤鈴木曾我之遺風也。其家素好古守義法律正直也。故世人稱之憲法。

The Yoshioka school of swordsmanship derived from the school practiced by Genbō Hideyuki, as well as the old Satō, Suzuki, and Soga fencing traditions. The house of Yoshioka was an ancient, law-abiding clan, for which reason the common people referred to its patriarch as Kenpō, or Justice.

It was Naomoto's brother, Naomitsu, who put the Yoshioka-*ryū* on the map when he became the personal fencing instructor to **Ashikaga Yoshiteru** (1536–65), known as the "master fencer *shōgun*." Naomitsu founded the Heihōsho, a large *dōjō* at Imadegawa, not far from the headquarters of the Ashikaga Bakufu. And while the Ashikaga Bakufu had long since fallen, by now, there was not a swordsman in the realm who did not know of the Yoshioka brothers and their prestigious school of fencing.

It is not surprising, then, that Musashi was keen to challenge the Yoshioka clan and its school of swordsmanship. Yet there was another important reason why Musashi picked the Yoshioka. According to the *Bukōden*, Musashi's father, Muni, had been invited to the capital by Ashikaga Yoshiaki (1537–97) to test his strength against his personal fencing instructor, Yoshioka Naokata, at that time considered to be the foremost swordsman in the realm:

曾て扶桑第一の劔術者、公方義照〔義昭〕公の師、洛陽の士、吉岡庄左衛門兼法と云。公方命にて無二と雌雄を決セしむ。限るに相交ル事参分を以す。吉岡一度利を得、無二兩同勝之。因て日下無雙兵法術者の號ヲ無二に賜ふ。

On orders of the shōgun a shiai was arranged between the two men. It was to be a bout in three rounds. The first round went to Kenpō, the second and third to Muni. And thus the title of hei-hōsha Without Equal Under the Heavens went to Muni.

For Musashi, a victory over even one of the members of the Yoshioka clan would have been not only a validation of the superiority of his own school of swordsmanship, but—perhaps even more importantly—concrete proof that he was at least his father's equal.

There is a lot of uncertainty surrounding the exact names of the Yoshioka swordsmen with whom Musashi dueled. According to the *Bushū denraiki* and the *Bukōden* Musashi dueled with three members of the Yoshioka clan who went by the names Seijurō, Denshichirō, and Matashichirō. The *Yoshioka-den*, however, mentions two men by the names of Genzaemon Naotsuna and Mataichi Naoshige. The *Koro usawa* only mentions a certain Yoshioka Kanefusa. The *Gekken sōdan* on the other hand speaks of a certain **Yoshioka Kenpō**, a name usually associated with the founder of the Yoshioka-*ryū*, Naomoto, but also used by many of his descendants. It is probably because of this uncertainty that the *Honchō bugei shōden* stays clear of calling the men by name and simply refers to them by their family name. Most historians now tentatively agree that the men's full names probably were Yoshioka Seijūrō Naotsuna, Yoshioka Denshichirō Naoshige, and Yoshioka Matashichirō, who at seventeen, had not yet reached adulthood and had therefore not yet received a given name.

Yoshioka Seijūrō Naotsuna

Both the *Bushū denraiki* and the *Bukōden* agree that the first member of the Yoshioka clan to duel with Musashi in the grounds of the Rendai temple on Kyoto's northern outskirts was Yoshioka Seijurō. The *Bushū denraiki* claims that:

武州、其日に至り病臥、起居不安の由にて、斷に及
ぶ。清十郎、頻に可致勝負旨、數度使を走らしむ。
武州竹輿に乘り、大夜着を着し、場所へ至らる。

When the day came Musashi excused himself as he was ill in bed. Sejirō now sent round messengers several times, strongly urging Musashi that he should fight. And thus Musashi mounted a palanquin and arrived at the appointed place wrapped in a futon.

It is widely assumed that Musashi's tardiness was not so much induced by any serious illness, but part of his strategy to unsettle his opponent. Yet according to the *Koro usawa*:

従者「いかに」といふに、「かちを考ふるに、いま
だ気不満。おしつけ出ん」とて、はかまかたきぬに
て北野に至る。

When asked by his attendant Musashi replied: "I am trying to think by what strategy I can gain victory, but I am not yet satisfied. I'll go presently."

The *Bukōden* claims that:

初吉岡兼法ガ嫡嗣清十良と、洛外蓮臺野に於て勝負
を決す。吉岡は眞劔也。武公木刀を以一度撃之。吉
岡斃て息絶ふ。豫め一撃の約あるに依て命根を輔弼
す。彼門生等板の上に助乘て家に帰、藥治浴湯して
本復す。

Seijūrō fought with a shinken. Musashi was armed with a bokutō, and struck out once. Seijūrō collapsed and lost consciousness. He was saved in that they had agreed only to attack once. The Yoshioka deshi placed him on a stretcher and took him home where they nursed him back to health.

Perhaps not surprisingly, this version of events is contradicted by the *Yoshioka-den*, which claims that:

於是直綱先出、兩方相支、互竭心力、暫移時刻、武
藏遂被擊眉間、血出最甚。直綱却後、皆言、「直綱
之勝也」。他言、「相擊也」。直綱怒云、「然則明
白一決」。武藏言、「與直綱已決了。所願與直重宜
相擊」。

Naotsuna was the first to step forward and match his skill with Musashi. Both men exerted their mental powers against each other, but already shortly into the bout Musashi was hit on the forehead and lost a lot of blood. When Naotsuna stepped back the crowd cried out that it had been Natsuna's victory. Yet others said that it had been a draw. Angered, Naotsuna said: "In that case, let us meet again in contest to make clear who is the winner." At this Musashi said: "My contest with Naotsuna is done. Now I want to fight with Mataichi Naoshige."

Though the *Honchō bugei shoden* does not mention the Yoshioka swordsman by name, it does give an interesting, more evenhanded, account of the duel:

武藏吉岡と仕相の事、武藏は柿手拭にて鉢巻す。吉
岡は白手拭にて鉢巻したり。吉岡が太刀武藏がひた
いに當る。武藏が太刀も又吉岡がひたひにあたるに
、吉岡は白手拭故血はやくみえ、武藏は柿てのごひ
故しばらくして血見ゆるとなり。吉岡大木刀を以て
武藏を打。武藏是を受るといへ共、鉢巻されて落た
り。武藏しづんで拂、木刀にて吉岡がきたる皮ばか
まをきる。吉岡は武藏が鉢巻を切て落し、武藏は吉
岡が袴を切る。何れも勝劣あるまじき達人と、見物
の耳目を驚かすと也。

During his duel with the Yoshioka Musashi wore a crimson hand cloth as hachimaki. The Yoshioka swordsman wore a hachimaki from a white hand cloth. Yoshioka hit Musashi on the brow with his tachi. And when Musashi, too, struck Yoshioka on the forehead, it was immediately visible, as he was wearing a white hachimaki, whereas on Musashi, because his hachimaki was crimson, it took some time before the blood on his forehead could be seen. Now Yoshioka struck Musashi with a long bokutō. Musashi parried the blow, but his hachimaki was torn and fell to the ground. Musashi now advanced on Yoshioka and cut through the leather hakama the latter was wearing. Thus Yoshioka cut through Musashi's hachimaki, and Musashi did the same with Yoshioka's hakama. It was a sight to behold, both dazzling to the eye and to the ear, and it was hard to say which of the two adepts had come out on top.

Yoshioka Denshichirō Naoshige

The *Kokura hibun* describes how:

吉岡傳七郎、又、洛外に出で、雌雄を決す。傳七、五尺餘の木双を袖して來たる。武藏、其の機に臨んで彼の木双を奪ひ、之を撃つ。地に伏して立所に死す。

Yoshioka Denshichirō, too, left Kyoto to fight it out with Musashi. He attacked him with a five-foot-long bokutō. Seizing the opportunity, Musashi wrested the bokutō from him and struck him with his own weapon, so that Denshichirō fell to the ground and expired.

This version of events is supported both by the *Bushū denraiki* and the *Bukōden*, which carry similar descriptions of the encounter, making it highly likely that both took their cue from the *Kokura hibun*. None of the records state where exactly the second duel took place, leading many historians to assume it must also have been on the Rendai plains.

Yoshioka Matashichirō

The last and the youngest Yoshioka scion to duel with Musashi was Yoshioka Matashichirō, although the *Kokura hibun* claims that his encounter with Musashi took the form of an ambush(see Musashi's Places). Thus the *Kokura hibun* describes how:

事を兵術に寄せ、洛外、下松邊りに彼の門生数百人を會し、兵伏弓箭を以て、忽ち之を害せんと欲す。

Matashichirō gathered his deshi and awaited Musashi in an ambush on the outskirts of Kyoto at Sagarimatsu. There were several hundreds of deshi, intending to kill Musashi in a single attack with swords, as well as bows and arrows.

Here too, the *Bushū denraiki* and the *Bukoden* closely follow the *Kokura hibun*, though the *Bukōden* adds that Matashichirō was Seijūrō's son and that they had gathered at Sagarimatsu "feigning to practice." The *Bushū denraiki*'s point of view focuses on Musashi, claiming he was back on the road (presumably satisfied with the outcome of his recent two duels), and was passing through Sagarimatsu in the company of a dozen of his "allies" when:

中にも十七八歳の若者、一番に進む。武州、跡より声をかけて、「加様の場にてたるめば命を墜すものぞ。少もたるむな」とて、後より帯を取て、真先に推立進まる。彼者矢に當て疵を被る。

A young man of seventeen or eighteen among them was way out ahead. Calling out to him from behind Musashi seized him by his belt and pushed him forward saying, "if you slacken your resolve here you will lose your life; remain firm." But the young man was struck by an arrow and wounded.

It goes in to describe how:

武州、門人等に曰、「何れも心閑かに立退き候へ。我等一人踏留り、大勢を追拂ひ、跡より可追付」とて、門人を先だて、多敵の位にて打拂々々退かる。

Musashi spoke out and addressed his followers, saying, "Stay calm and move back, you can catch up with me once I have driven them back." At this, he stepped out in front of his followers and, using his tateki no i proceeded to drive the enemy back.

It claims that, the road ahead being blocked by hundreds of Matashichirō's henchmen, Musashi fled to a "temple," where he hid himself, until at length the disturbance was subdued with the help of the *shoshidai*, the head of the Samurai Dokoro. It is not clear which temple the *Bushū denraiki* is referring to, although two nearby temples that lay derelict at the time are possible contenders (see Musashi's Places).

This version of events is somewhat less heroic than that given in the *Bukōden*, as well as the *Kokura hibun*, which claim that Musashi "scattered his enemies apart" so that "it seemed as if a wild dog was chasing away wild beasts."

* *The Samurai Dokoro (侍所) was a remnant of the Kamakura and Muromachi periods. Founded in 1180, it initially functioned as a disciplinary board that controlled the vassals of Minamoto no Yoritomo (1147–99). During the Muromachi period, its duties grew to include administration of shōgunal property and the policing of Kyoto, which was then still the capital. Though the Samurai Dokoro was abolished not long after the founding of the Edo Bakufu, the function of deputy governor with its responsibility of keeping order in Kyoto remained.*

Sasaki Kojirō

The best documented and perhaps therefore most celebrated of Musashi's many duels is undoubtedly that with the ace swordsman **Sasaki Kojirō**. Kojirō was not just any wandering swordsman. At a young age, he is said to have entered the service of the powerful Asakura clan, which had its headquarters of Ichijōdani castle. The Asakura were known as great patrons of the martial arts, especially of the Toda school of fencing, which traced its ancestry way back to the legendary fifteenth-century warrior-monk Nenami Jion and his Nen school of fencing.

Chief propagator of the Toda-*ryū* in Kojiro's day was the famous Toda Seigen, who had under his wing a large number of aspiring swordsmen, including his star *deshi* Yamazaki

Rokusaemon (who was later adopted by the Toda and given the name Toda Shigemasa), and Kanemaki Jisai. It was probably under Jisai that Kojirō acquired many of the Toda techniques, although, according to the *Bukōden*:

小次郎、幼少より勢源が打太刀を勤め、勢源は一尺
五寸の木太刀を以、三尺の刀に對し、勝事を爲す。
小次郎、常に三尺を以、勢源に對て粗技能あり。因
て十八歳の時師の前を欠落し、自劍一流を立て、岩
流と号。

From a young age, Kojirō served Seigen in the role of uchidachi. Wielding a tantō of one-and-a-half feet long, Seigen would win bouts against opponents with swords of three feet in length. But already at this young age, when fighting with the long sword, Kojirō was almost Seigen's equal. And thus, at the age of eighteen, Kojirō left Seigen's service to establish his own school of swordsmanship, which he gave the name Ganryū.

* *The Nitenki claims that he was only eighteen when he dueled with Musashi, even though its precursor, the Bukōden, clearly states this was the age at which he founded his Gan-ryū.*

Following the destruction of the Asakura clan by Oda Nobunaga's forces in 1573 Kojiro embarked on a *musha shugyō* until, in 1610, in his early fifties, he became a fencing instructor to Hosokawa Tadaoki (1563–1646). The *Bukōden* claims that it was at this juncture that:

武公、從都来［慶長十七年壬子二十九歳］、故長岡佐
渡興長の第に到て、請て曰［興長嘗武公の父無二の門
弟なり］、「曾て聞、小次郎劍術奇絶なりと。庶幾我
手技を比ん事を。公は家父無二ガ故あり、因て可憑て
来者也。謹で願ふ、達せられん事を」と。

Musashi came down from the capital (in the seventeenth year of Keichō, at the age of twenty-eight) and stayed at the yashiki of Nagaoka Okinaga, who had once been a deshi to Musashi's father, Munisai, and said to him, "I hear that Kojirō's art of swordsmanship is exceedingly rare and I would like to meet him in duel. It is only because you were once connected to my father that I now ask that you enable this contest to go forth."

* *Nagaoka (also Matsui) Okinaga (1582–1661)was a high-ranking vassal of Lord Hosokawa Tadaoki. He was the second son of Nagaoka Yasuyuki (1550–1612), the lord of Kitsuki castle, in the neighboring province of Bungo (see Musashi's Places). Okinaga and Musashi had first met and both fought in the Battle of Ishigakihara and the numerous sieges that followed, notably, the siege of Tomiku castle (see Musashi's Battles).*

It was through Okinaga's offices, then, that, sometime in the summer of 1612, in the first third of the hour of the Dragon (7:00–7:40), Musashi and Kojirō met in duel on the small, remote island, situated a few miles sailing to the east from Kokura in the Straits of Shimonoseki. Little more than a raised sandbank, it lay on the border of Buzen and Nagato provinces, and was known variously as Funashima or Mukōjima, although today it is better known as Ganryū-jima.

The various sources differ on which of the two swordsmen arrived at the island first. Whereas the *Bukōden* claims that Kojirō was the first to arrive at the island, the *Bushū denraiki*, holds that it was Musashi who first set foot on the island. Predictably, given the outcome of the bout, both scenarios are made to work in Musashi's favor, according to the former because he caused his opponent to lose patience, according to the latter because he could dictate events. Remarkably, the *Kokura hibun*, on which both works seem to rely a great deal, claims that both men met on the island "at the same time."

There are other, more pertinent differences between these two versions of events. While the *Bushū denraiki* claims that the event was witnessed by Hosokawa Tadaoki's son, Tadatoshi, (then still lord of Moji castle, north of Kokura), the *Bukōden* only mentions Lord Tadaoki's *kenshi* or "inspectors."

No mention is made of Tadaoki's son. Instead, it mentions that Musashi was chased off the island by Hosokawa retainers riled by the outcome of the bout. Though these may have been Kojirō's *deshi*, it seems unlikely since, according to the same source, Tadaoki had strictly forbidden anyone to observe or participate in the duel.

There is less disagreement on the duel itself. Both sources have Kojirō open the attack. According to the *Bukōden* "he struck out at Musashi's brow, cutting the knot in the latter's head towel, which fell to the ground." According to the *Bushū denraiki* he attacked Musashi "by striking left and right with his two-feet-seven-inch-long Aoe sword using a *mizukuruma* technique, without turning his head."

* *The famous* mizukuruma, *or "water mill," technique employed by Kojirō evokes an image in which the swordsman boldly brandishes his sword in a large, rotating fashion, but this is not necessarily so. Traditional Japanese water mills do not merely consist of a single wheel that scoops up the water, but of a conveyor belt-like chain of buckets mounted at one side on an axis, and on the other side on a large wheel that is driven by one or more footmen. The action of the water mill consists of a sweeping motion in which the water is first driven along in front of the buckets through a wooden gutter after which it is scooped up as the buckets rise one by one on the large wheel. In the* mizukuruma *technique, then, the sword is similarly swept close along the ground and then brought up in a large, circular motion akin to that of the rising water buckets. This is borne out by the fact that most accounts claim that Musashi's* hakama *was cut in the duel. The image that arises, then, is one in which Kojirō strikes at Musashi with his sword in two large upward motions, first toward the left and then toward the right.*

Both sources state that Musashi was fighting with a *bokutō* he had crafted from a wooden oar. They also confirm that his improvised weapon struck Kojirō's head, causing him to fall. Yet they differ on Musashi's subsequent moves: The *Bushū denraiki* (which still refers to Musashi by his infant name of Bennosuke) claims that:

辨之助、二の目を打んと立よる所を、小次郎ふつと起あがり、両膝をしきながら、横に拂ふ。辨之助が、るさんの前をはらりと切放て、かるさん前に垂る。辨之助、二の目を又したゝかに打つ。大力の然も舟の櫂のしたゝかなるを以て、同じつぼを二つ迄打たる故、頭碎けてひれ臥せり。

When Bennosuke moved in for the second strike Kojirō quickly rose to his knees and struck out horizontally, tearing through Bennosuke's hakama. Bennosuke's second strike, however, was a fierce one. Striking twice at the same spot with all his might the sturdy bokutō he had crafted from the oar crushed the skull and Kojirō slumped forward and lay prostrate.

The *Bukōden*, by contrast, claims that:

武公木刀を堤て暫く立、亦振上て打たんとす。小次郎臥ながら打拂ふ。武公が・たる袴衣の裾の膝の上に垂たる所を、三寸許剪り落す。同武公が木刀、小次良が脇の下の横骨を打折て、即ち氣絶す。

Musashi lowered his oar and stood there for some time before he raised it to strike out again. But Kojirō, who was still lying down, struck out at Musashi's legs, cutting away some three inches of the hakama he had tied up above his knees. But already Musashi's oar had struck his opponent in the side, causing his hip to break under the impact and Kojirō to pass out.

A widely diverging—and far less heroic—version of events is given by the *Numata kaki*. The family records of the Numata clan, the *Numata kaki* was compiled in 1672 by a descendant of Numata Nobumoto, the keeper of Moji castle, situated some ten miles northwest of Kokura. Going against most other records, it claims that:

小次郎は如兼弟子一人も不参候、武蔵弟子共参り隠れ居申候、其後に小次郎蘇生致候得共　彼弟子共参合　後にて打殺申候。

Kojirō had not brought along any deshi, as he had promised, but Musashi's deshi had come to the island and hid themselves. Following the duel Kojirō regained consciousness, yet Musashi's deshi ganged in on him and killed him.

Though it confirms that Musashi won the duel, it throws a different light on Kojirō's death. It also is the one record to describe how, like his behavior following the Yoshioka ambush at Sagarimatsu, Musashi sought to escape the followers of those he had slain in duel. Thus it describes how that:

依之武蔵難遁門司に遁来、延元様を偏に奉願候に付御請合被成、則城中へ被召置候に付、武蔵無恙運を開申候。

In order to avoid trouble, Musashi fled to Moji castle, seeking the help of master Nobumoto, who acquiesced and gave Musashi shelter at his castle, so that the latter was spared.

* *There is still much uncertainty around Kojirō's name. The Kokura hibun merely mentions the man was called Ganryū. The Numata kaki refers to him as "a man by the name of Kojirō who used the Gan-ryū method of combat." The Bukōden identifies him as Ganryū Kojirō. So does its spin-off the Nitenki, although, surprisingly, the latter also uses the name Sasaki Kojirō. The family name of Sasaki occurs in a number of other works that appeared during the eighteenth century, leading some to believe his real name must indeed have been Sasaki Kojirō. This still does not give us absolute certainty. The Bushū denraiki and the Heihō senshi denki, for instance, mention the family name of Tsuda. Indeed, some Japanese scholars believe the name Sasaki Kojirō may have been an invention of the early eighteenth-century kabuki playwrights, who gave their villain such varying names as Sasaki Ganryū, Ganryū Kojirō, or Sasaki Kojirō.*

MUSASHI'S BOUTS

There are far more recorded friendly bouts than life and death duels involving Musashi. Given that Musashi himself was very reticent about the events of his life, let alone his sixty deadly duels, it is perhaps not surprising that we know far more about his friendly encounters than those in which his opponents were killed. The dead, after all, do not talk, and it seems unlikely that the followers of his victims felt the urge to publicly recall the humiliating defeat of their master and thereby tacitly acknowledge the inferiority of the school of *heihō* they practiced.

Many of his opponents in these more-or-less friendly encounters, on the other hand, were either already among his *deshi*, or became his pupils in the wake of their defeat. Being practitioners of Musashi's school of swordsmanship, they would have had few qualms in recounting their defeat at the master's hand. Indeed, they would have taken great pride in having personally "dueled" with a man considered to be invincible by many—and certainly by those who practiced Musashi's art of swordsmanship.

Thus the *Bushū denraiki* describes how, following a match in which he momentarily managed to break Musashi's defense, the Hōzōin-*ryū* practitioner **Takada Matabei Yoshitsugu** addresses the gathered crowd (which included Lord Ogasawara Tadazane), saying:

武州が兵法は、中々我等などが段式にてはなし。申たり共、各合点行まじ。三本目當りたりと武州はいへど、吾は曽て覚へず。當時の挨拶たるべし。至極の達人、言語にうたらず。

Musashi's attainment of the art of heihō *is on another par with mine, although nobody understands it, even if I say so. Musashi claims that I struck him the third time round, but I have no recollection of doing so. It must have been his good manners that caused him to say so. His genius is beyond in words.*

It should also not surprise us that all of the friendly matches that have been recorded took place long after Musashi's last recorded kill in a duel, i.e., his slaying of Sasaki Kojirō on Funajima Island in 1612. With age he seems to have lost much of his youthful rage, content to drive his point home without necessarily doing so at the cost of his opponent's life. As such he had come a long way since the time he bludgeoned Arima Kihei to death with a succession of fourteen to fifteen blows to the head.

What is certain is that Musashi himself did not regard these encounters as duels. In the opening paragraphs of the *Chi no maki* (Earth Scroll) of his *Gorin no sho*, he mentions that the sixty duels he fought all took place before his twenty-seventh year. This can only mean that he saw the many matches in which he engaged later in life in a different light, even though many chroniclers did prefer to use the word duel. He probably considered them either practice bouts, meant to hone his skills and those of his many followers, or friendly matches, simple tests of strength designed to demonstrate the superiority of his school of swordsmanship.

Miyake Gunbei/Gundayū

The only recorded match during Musashi's brief stay at Himeji (though he probably spent much of his time in Hirafuku with his mother and his adopted son Mikinosuke) was with a certain Miyake Gunbei or Gundayū, a practitioner of the Tōgun school of swordsmanship.

** The Tōgun-ryū was founded by Kawasaki Kaginosuke, the son of Kawasaki Tokisada, who had been in the service of the illustrious Asakura. At a young age, Kaginosuke studied the art of swordsmanship under none other than Toda Seigen, chief propagator of the Toda-ryū, the official school of swordsman-*

ship of the Asakura clan. Following the demise of the Asakura Kaginosuke had led the life of a rōnin, until he was taken in by Tōgun Sōjō, abbot of the Hiezan monastery near Kyoto. Kaginosuke continued his study of the art of swordsmanship under Sōjō, naming his school after the Hiezan monk.

According to the *Bisan hōkan*, Gundayū was sent by **Honda Tadamasa**, the lord of Himeji castle, to test Musashi's skill and see if he was suitable to enter his lordship's service. It describes how Musashi makes the retainer wait in the anteroom of his house until the latter loses his temper and insists on a match. During that match:

武蔵は木刀を揮って庭で試合した。軍太夫、敵する能わず、三宅は頭を下げて、武蔵の大言壮語、「日本第一」の号を自称するのも、当然だとして、帰って主君本多忠政に報告した。

Musashi wielded a bokutō as they faced each other off in the garden. However, Miyake was no match for him and dropped his head in defeat. Thus he returned to Lord Honda Tadamasa, reporting that Musashi's boastful claim that he was the greatest swordsman in the realm was only rightful.

Interestingly, the *Nihon kendō-shi*, published in 1925, also features Musashi's meeting with a man with the surname Miyake, followed by a match in the garden of Musashi's dwelling. In this version, however, the man's given name is Gunbei, and not Gundayū. It describes how Gunbei opens the attack and Musashi gradually retreats until:

丁度戸口を負つてはや下がるべき餘地がない。爰なりと軍兵衛は三太刀目は取込んで突きを入れようと、木刀を中取にして韋駄天の如く突かくるを、此時疾し、武蔵は危ないと掛聲して、左の小太刀で軍兵衛の頬を突いた。鮮血が迸って、自分の直進の勢い

にかえって身を傷つけられたのに、軍兵衛が閉口し
たのを、武蔵は微笑して、「まず、血を拭え」と控
えて居る。

Musashi had his back against the entrance and had no more room to back away. Convinced he had Musashi cornered Gunbei now lowered his bokutō and drew the weapon back to run him through the third time round, when Musashi shouted, "Look out," and stabbed him in the face with his short bokutō. Gunbei's jaw dropped as fresh blood gushed forward from the wound inflicted by the vigor of his own thrust. Musashi laughed and held back saying, "First wipe this blood away."

The *Nihon kendō-shi* is not clear on where exactly Musashi was staying when the two men encountered. More importantly, Miyake, in this version of events, is not a retainer of Honda Tadamasa, but of his son, **Honda Masatomo** (1599–1638), at that time the *daimyō* of the neighboring fiefdom of Tatsuno, which was situated a few miles west of Himeji.

Apart from the fact that the *Nihon kendō-shi* was only compiled in 1925, some three decades after the *Bisan hōkan*, there are several reasons why it seems unlikely that Musashi should have had a match with one of Masatomo's retainers. For one, it is hard to imagine that Masatomo's retainers would have an interest—or the liberty—to challenge Musashi if he were staying in Himeji. The Himeji domain, after all, fell under the jurisdiction of Masatomo's father, Tadamasa. They would have had even less authority to do so had Musashi been staying with his stepmother in Hirafuku. The fiefdom of Hirafuku at the time belonged to Ikeda Teruoki, one of the few members of the Ikeda clan who had been allowed to hang on to their possessions in Harima with the redistribution of territories in the wake of Ikeda Mitsumasa's demotion to the fiefdom of Tottori.

Musō Gonnosuke Katsuyoshi

Remarkably, there is also just one recorded match during Musashi's fourteen-year-long stay at Akashi (from 1618 to 1632): the match with **Musō Gonnosuke Katsuyoshi**, an adept with the *jō*, or wooden staff. Gonnosuke had studied Iizasa Chōissai Ienao's famous Shōden Katori Shintō-*ryū* under Sakurai Yoshikatsu. According to the school's own chronicles his clan name was Yamamoto and his given name or *imina* (諱) was Katsuyoshi. Other sources claim he belonged to the Hirano clan and that his common name was Gonbei.

Though living in Akashi at the time of his match with Musashi, Gonnosuke probably went on to enter the service of **Kuroda Nagamasa**, the *daimyō* of the Fukuoka fiefdom in the province of Chikuzen, where his school of *jōjutsu* was passed on throughout the Edo period. It is believed that, during a period of meditation and abstinence of thirty-seven days on nearby Mount Hōman, he had a revelation in which he was approached by a young boy with the words *maruki wo motte, suigetsu wo shire* (丸木を以って、水月を知れ), "know your opponent's weak points by means of the round wood." After yet more meditation and study he went on to found his own school of *jōjutsu*, naming it the Shintō Musō-*ryū*.

* *The term* suigetsu *has many meanings and connotations in Japanese. Literally meaning the reflection of the moon on the surface of the water, it represents the bodiless nature of illusion. As such it was embodied by one of the thirty-three* kannon. *In medieval military tactics, it stood for a battlefield in which both armies opposed each other in perfect symmetry. In the martial arts, however, it stood for the vital points on the human body (at which to strike), specifically the solar plexus.*

The *Kaijō monogatari* recounts how Gonnosuke visited Musashi at his *yashiki* in Akashi to challenge him to a friendly bout. After a lengthy argument Musashi finally gives in and:

権之介、透間なく打てかゝる。武蔵、かの木ぎれを以て、ちよつちよつととめて、太刀を出させず。権之介、太刀をかへして、なぐりければ、武蔵が袖の下、羽織のえりに、木刀のさき打当る。此時権之介、高声に、「あたれり。あたれり」と云。武蔵聞て、「いや、かように当をあたりたるとはいはず。かようにあたつて何の用にたらむや。さらば、我当て見せ申さむ」と云て、又打合せける。権之介、随分うたむとおもふ気色面にあらはれて、打てかゝりけれ共、太刀を出す事不叶、覚はず志さりけり。むさし、座敷の隅に追つめ、ひしと眉間を打つ。俄に色付はれ上りたり。爰にをゐて権之介、大に悲をしり、弟子と成也。

Gonnosuke immediately charged with his staff, but each time, Musashi stopped him with a few light parries of a piece of willow. Gonnosuke now changed the grip on his staff and struck out with a horizontal blow, touching the collar of Musashi's haori just below his sleeve. He cried out in a loud voice: "I struck you! I struck you!" But Musashi said: "No! One cannot call that a strike. What good would such a strike do? Let me show you what a real strike is." Gonnosuke grew red in the face as he concentrated on an opening in Musashi's defense, but he failed to find one and suddenly found himself veering backward. Musashi had driven Gonnosuke into a corner of the room and had landed a fierce blow on his forehead, which immediately swelled red. Gonnosuke acknowledged defeat and, regretting his folly, became Musashi's deshi.

The school's own records claim that, following his defeat at Musashi's hands, Gonnosuke withdrew to the ancient Kamado shrine on Mount Hōman for meditation and reflection. When he finally came out of his self-imposed exile, Gonnosuke is said to have challenged Musashi to a second match in which he did claim victory.

In yet another version of the encounter, the *Nitenki* claims that Gonnosuke challenged Musashi when he was still living in Edo and that Musashi struck him down with a single blow.

Tokugawa Yoshinao's Swordsmen

Some of Musashi's friendly bouts were the result of an invitation by a feudal lord to demonstrate his art of swordsmanship. One of the most high-ranking men to attend such a demonstration was **Tokugawa Yoshinao** (1601–50), the *daimyō* of Owari. The ninth son of Tokugawa Ieyasu, Yoshinao had been only fourteen years old when he took part in the siege of Osaka castle, attending his father's camp during the winter campaign and leading reinforcements during the Battle of Tennōji (1615).

From a young age, Yoshinao had taken a profound interest in the martial arts. Like his father he patronized the Yagyū Shinkage school of swordsmanship. His chief fencing instructor was Yagyū Toshiyoshi, the nephew of the famed **Yagyū Munenori**. In his youth, Yoshinao had submitted himself to five years of intensive practice under Toshiyoshi's guidance and had grown into a highly accomplished swordsman.

The *Mukashibanashi* describes how, in the fall of 1632:

宮本武蔵がなごやへ来りしを召され、於御前兵法つ
かひ仕合せし時、相手すつと立合と、武蔵くみたる
二刀のま丶、大の切先を相手の鼻のさきへつけて、
一間のうちを一ぺんまわしあるきて、勝負如此二御
座候と申上し。

Miyamoto Musashi was invited to Nagoya to demonstrate his art of swordsmanship in his lordship's presence, when his oppo-

nent suddenly opened the attack. But Musashi crossed his two swords, trained the tip of his long sword on his adversary's nose, and steadily forced him back until they had traced the circumference of the whole dōjō. Then he said, "this is the way in which I fight duels."

Yoshinao was probably the only member of the illustrious Tokugawa clan to ever see Musashi in action. Two decades earlier, when Musashi was still living in Edo, he had been invited by none other than **Tokugawa Ieyasu** himself to give a demonstration of his art at Edo castle. According to the *Bushū denraiki*:

武州兵法、將軍家達上聞、可被召出御沙汰ありとい
へ共、柳生但馬守殿、御師範として常住御前に侍席
せらる。武州、柳生が下に立ん事を忌て、「若年よ
り仕官の望なく、髪剃ず、爪とらず、法外の有様也
。御免を奉蒙度」旨達て御断申上らる。

The shōgunal house had taken notice of Musashi's art of heihō and word was sent to Musashi that they wanted to invite him. Lord Yagyū Tajima no Kami Munenori, however, was already serving the Bakufu as shōgunal shihan. Musashi railed at the thought of being placed below the Yagyū saying, "From my youth I have held no ambitions for high office, and with my hair and nails uncut I would cut a strange figure, so please forgive me for declining."

* *It had been a similar occasion that led to Yagyū Muneyoshi's ascendancy. In the early summer of 1594, Ieyasu was encamped at Takagamine, on the bank of the Kamo River, on the northern outskirts of Kyoto, when (through Kuroda Nagamasa) he sent for the Yagyū chieftain to come and give a demonstration of the Yagyū Shinkage school of swordsmanship. Muneyoshi did so in style. Ieyasu's senior by fourteen years, the warrior disarmed the great shōgun in a brilliant performance of mutōtori, a technique by which one can wrest a weapon from*

one's opponent without using one's sword. Impressed with Muneyoshi's performance, Ieyasu appointed the swordsman as his personal fencing instructor, or shōgun shihan (将軍師範), a position that became hereditary within the Yagyū clan.

Matusdaira Katsutaka

One of the more important men to have a friendly match with Musashi when he was in his fifties was Matsudaira Katsutaka. Matsudaira Katsutaka (1589–1666) was the son of Matsudaira Shigekatsu (1549–1621), one of Ieyasu's most senior vassals, who had held a string of important positions within the Bakufu. In 1634 Katsutaka had moved down to the island of Shikoku to take up temporary residence on the grounds of Iyo Matsuyama castle. The former lord of **Matsuyama castle** had passed away and the Bakufu had decided that henceforth the Matsuyama domain was to be governed by a member of the Matsudaira, the clan from which the Tokugawa themselves descended. It was Katsutaka's duty to prepare the *hikiwatashi*, the castle's smooth transfer from one clan to another.

It was probably on his way south by boat across the Inland Sea to join his son in Kokura (the fiefdom to which his master, Ogasawara Tadazane had just been promoted), that Musashi visited Katsutaka at Matsuyama. Katsutaka's clan, after all, was related to the Ogasawara (Tadazane's fourth son was adopted by Katsutaka's eldest brother), and it is very likely that he and Musashi had met at Akashi or Kokura castle, and that Katsutaka had invited the swordsman to pay him a visit.

Thus the *Bushū denraiki* records that, "In the era of Kan'ei [1624–44] Musashi stayed at the house of lord Matsudaira Izumo no Kami." To be true to the text, the *Bushū denraiki* only speaks of Matsudaira Izumo no Kami. This has led a number of authors (most notably Yoshikawa Eiji in his novel *Musashi*) to claim that Musashi was the guest of Matsudaira

Naomasa (1601–1666), the grandson of Tokugawa Ieyasu and the lord of Matsue castle. Matsue castle, after all, is located in what once was the province of Izumo, leading them to assume that the honorific title of "Izumo no Kami" must have referred to its master, Matsudaira Naomasa. This, however, is to ignore the fact that it was Matsudaira Katsutaka (1589–1666) who bore the title of Izumo no Kami, and not Naomasa (whose honorific title was Dewa no Kami).

Another strong indication that the event was not staged at **Matsue castle** but at Matsuyama is the fact that the same record states that Musashi "stayed at the house of Lord Matsudaira Izumo no Kami," (*Matsudaira Izumo no Kami no ie ni ari*), rather than the castle's stately mansion (*goten*), which would logically have been the case had he been the guest of Lord Naomasa, the master of Matsue castle. If, therefore, Musashi's host was Katsutaka and not Naomasa, the match would have been held somewhere in the vicinity of Matsuyama castle, where Katsutaka would have stayed in an official accommodation, rather than at the lord's palace within the castle grounds.

The *Bushū denraiki* describes how, on Katsutaka's request, Musashi engaged with one of his retainers in the library garden but that, "Musashi struck out hard at the man's left and rigth-hand wrists, and as he faltered, struck him down and claimed victory." It goes on to describe how, against the advice of his councilors, Katsutaka took his place opposite Musashi and that:

武州は二刀にて、三度まで追込まる。三度目には床の上に追上たり。雲州、尚もひるまず、又、木刀を振直されしを、直に付合、子ばりをかけて、石火のあたりにて、したゝかに當らる。木刀二つに折れて、一つは天井を打拔たり。

Up to three times Musashi drove Lord Izumo back with his three swords, the third time right into the library. But still Lord Izumo did not falter and when he sought to drive his weapon home Musashi intercepted the bokutō with his own using a nebari o kakuru, and then struck out at Lord Izumo's bokutō by means of a sekka no atari with all his might. This caused Lord Izumo's bokutō to break in two and one piece to hit the library's ceiling.

* *The two techniques of* nebari o kakuru *(applying glue) and* sekka no atari *(the spark-of-the-flint blow) are described in the Water Scroll (Mizu no maki) of the Book of Five Rings. "When the opponent parries your attack with a tachi,"* Musashi writes: *"keep your sword firmly against his, as if they had been glued together." The term "gluing," is meant "to convey the intent of keeping the swords together and that you should not go in with too much force. When one parries an opponent's sword in this way it does not matter how gently it is done." Musashi goes on to point out that "gluing" should not be confused with getting entangled with one's opponent. "Gluing is strong, but getting entangled is weak. It is necessary to distinguish between the two." Sekka no atari, by contrast, is a technique in which one "strikes the opponent's sword the moment when one's own sword and that of one's opponent are about to touch without even slightly raising one's sword." In this technique "it is important to strike quickly, while observing three points: a firm stance, a firm posture, and a firm grip."*

Ogawa Gondayū Rōshin

Like Musashi's mother, Ogawa (also Ogō) Gondayū Rōshin's clan hailed from Harima Province. Gondayū's grandfather had been a senior retainer or *karō* (家老) to Kodera Masamoto (1529–84), at that time a powerful warlord, who contended with the Bessho and the Akamatsu for influence in the region. When, in 1580, the Kodera were overrun by Oda Nobunaga, many of their retainers joined ranks with the Kuroda, a clan with whom they were closely related. When Gondayū's uncle fell in the Korean campaign, his father, Kanzaemon, became the head of the Ogawa clan and moved to Kyushu when Kuroda Nagamasa (1568–1623) was promoted to the Fukuoka fiefdom in the province of Chikuzen.

Gondayū was Kanzaemon's eldest son and entered Lord Nagamasa's service at a young age. When, in 1623, Nagamasa was succeeded by his eldest son, **Kuroda Tadayuki (1602–54)**, Gondayū fell out with his new master and was forced to leave Fukuoka. He moved to the port of Kitsuki, where he entered the service of Ogasawara Tadatomo (1599–1663). Tadatomo was the brother of Ogasawara Tadazane (see Musashi's Benefactors). In 1632 he had become the *daimyō* of Kitsuki when his brother was promoted to the fiefdom of Kokura.

Gondayū might have first met Musashi at Kitsuki, though it would not have been through Musashi's father, since Muni probably died sometime during the preceding decade (see Musashi's Father). It is more likely that they met in Kokura, where Musashi was staying with his son, Iori, who had by now become one of Tadazane's senior retainers.

It is no coincidence that we know so much about Gondayū, for Tanji Hōkin, the author of the *Bushū denraiki*, was the grandson of Gondayū's sister. Gondayū's anecdotes, then, would have been passed on by his sister to her children and grandchildren. Indeed, Hōkin might well have heard them directly from the mouth of his uncle. Thus Hōkin recounts how:

露心、常々物語に、「我等杯、若かりし時は、命を捨る事、屑ともせず。武州と立合、打太刀を致、「己、一太刀可打」と思儲け、木刀をし取立向ふ。武州、二刀を取、大太刀を杖につき、肩をくはつとくつろげらる、と、肝にこタへ、踏掛たる足を一足は必引たり。是、露心に不限、何れとても同然たり。武州が事は、咄したりとも、中々合点行まじ」と語れり。

Rōshin would often say "when I was young I did not give a damn about laying down my life. When I met with Musashi I challenged him to a duel. I thought 'I will give him a thrashing' and, seizing my bokutō, I went for him. Musashi simply took his two bokutō and leaning on the long bokutō he relaxed his wide shoulders with a flick of his muscles. At this, I grew timid and almost by instinct I drew back the very leg with which I had sought to advance. It was not just with me but the same with everyone. Yet, however much I talk, it is nigh on impossible to make people understand what Musashi was really like."

Takada Matabei Yoshitsugu

Takada Matabei Yoshitsugu (1590–1671) was a famous warrior who hailed from the province of Iga (today's Mie prefecture). Born in the village of Shirakashi (today part of Ueno city), he moved to Nara at a young age to study the art of fighting with the lance under Nakamura Ichiemon Naomasa (1583–1652), one of the star *deshi* of the great Hōzōin Inei (1521–1607), the famous abbot of the Kōfuku temple and the founder of the Hōzōin school of spear fighting.

It is believed that in his twenties Matabei moved to Edo to open his own *dōjō*, attracting more than four thousand followers. In 1623, at the age of thirty-four, he entered the service of Ogasawara Tadazane, then still the lord of **Akashi castle** in Harima. Like Musashi's son, Iori, Matabei moved down with lord Tadazane to Kokura on the southern island of Kyushu, and participated in the siege of Hara castle during the Shimabara rebellion.

Given that Matabei's stay at Akashi and later at Kokura coincided with that of Musashi, it is almost certain that he and Musashi practiced together regularly, although there would have been many *dōjō* in Akashi and Kokura. It was during Musashi's time in Kokura that, according to the *Bushū denraiki*, he and Matabei engaged in a friendly duel in the presence of Lord Tadazane. The record describes how:

武州は常の使ひ木刀二刀にて立合る。又兵衛、十文字の竹刀にて立向ふ。武州、中段の位にて三本迄入込る。三本目の時、「今のは當りたり。然れ共、下りて足に當れり」との玉ふ。見物の面々も見留めざるとも。

Musashi was armed with his inseparable two bokutō, while Matabei faced him with a cross-shaped yari made of bamboo. Up to three times Musashi charged, his bokutō held in a chūdan position. The third time round, he said: "This time I touched you, but the tip of your yari deflected, striking my leg." It seems that this had even escaped those who had been looking on.

* *The* chūdan, *or middle position is the first of Musashi's five* kamae *of* chūdan, jōdan, gedan, hidari no waki, *and* migi no waki, *all stances in which one awaits an attack in a defensive position, ready to parry and strike at any given moment. They are set out in detail in the Water Scroll (*Mizu no maki*), the second chapter of Musashi's Book of Five Rings. "In the chū-dan no kamae", Musashi explains, "one points the tip of one's tachi to his face. When the enemy strikes, deflect his long sword to the right and press on." It seems that this is exactly what Musashi did with Yoshitsugu's yari, causing it to hit his right leg.*

A similar anecdote is recorded in the *U no mane*. A late Edo chronicle by Kojima Yoshishige, a retainer from the Kokura fiefdom, it claims that Musashi and Matabei regularly practiced together and that the old master even advised the lancer on the type of weapon he should use.

Matabei's generous recognition of Musashi's superiority as portrayed in the *Bushū denraiki* stands in shrill contrast with an episode recorded in the *Heihō senshi denki*. Recorded by

Niwa Nobuhide (1726–91), a practitioner of Both Musashi's Niten Ichi-*ryū* and Inei's Hōzōin-*ryū*, it describes how, at one stage, Matabei visited the Edo *yashiki* of **Tokugawa Yorinobu** (1602–1671), the tenth son of Tokugawa Ieyasu, founder of the Tokugawa *Bakufu*.

Matabei had been sent to deliver a message on behalf of his master, Lord Tadazane, but Yorinobu's councilor **Andō Naotsugu** (1555–1635) insisted that he demonstrate his skill in a *shiai* with one of their own adepts with the *yari*. Matabei declined but after several entreaties finally gave in. Following several bouts he stepped back, content that all of them had been decided in his favor, when his opponent unexpectedly reopened the attack, cutting Matabei's sleeve and claiming victory. The record goes on to describe how "Matabei drew his *wakizashi*, pierced his sleeve and thundered "will anyone die if their sleeve is pierced?"

Takagi Umanosuke Shigesada

One of the more enigmatic opponents in Musashi's friendly bouts was a man by the name of Takagi Umanosuke Shigesada, a practitioner of an unarmed martial art employing various grappling techniques that came to be known as the Hontai Yōshin-*ryū*. According to the *Bushū denraiki*:

寛永の比、毛利家の士に高木右馬允と云多力の者あり。叡聞に達し、禁庭に召して、力量叡覧有しに、重目百五十貫目を持つ。

During the Kan'ei era [1624–44] there was an incredibly strong man by the name of Takagi Umanosuke, who served the house of Mōri as a retainer. One day the emperor heard of this and summoned him to the forbidden gardens. There, under the emperor's watchful eyes, he lifted a weight of 150 kan.

It was long believed that the **Takagi Umanosuke** in question was the son of Takagi Shigetoshi, alias Takagi Oriemon, widely believed to have been the founder of the Takagi school of *jūjutsu*. However, Oriemon was born in 1625, while his son, Umanosuke (though spelled in the same way, yet written as 馬之輔 and not 右馬助) was born in 1656 and died in 1717. Given that Musashi died in 1645, this Umanosuke could impossibly have met with Musashi.

* *Like Umanosuke, Oriemon also seems to have been known for his extraordinary strength. One anecdote recounts how, on one of his* musha shugyū, *Oriemon was among the mountains when he was surrounded by a gang of robbers. When their leader charged him with a heavy iron rod, Oriemon, seized the rod, wrestled the man to the ground, and bent it around his neck. Years later, while languishing at the Arima hot springs near Kobe, he spotted an old man entering the steaming water with a rusted piece of iron around his neck. When he approached the man, it turned out to be the robber he had encountered among the mountains. The man had repented and become an itinerant monk, wearing his iron collar as a constant reminder of his past sins. Overcome by pity Oriemon took hold of both ends of the collar and freed the man by breaking it open.*

More recent research suggests that Takagi Umanosuke was probably a former retainer of Mori Tadamasa (1570–1634), *daimyō* of the Tsuyama fief in Mimasaka. Tadamasa was a troubled man. In 1626, his twenty-two-year-old son, Tadahiro, had married Kametsuruhime, the adopted daughter of *shōgun* **Tokugawa Hidetada**. For Tadamasa it was a ticket for a seat at the *shōgun*'s court. But in 1630, at the young age of seventeen, Kametsuruhime died without having borne any children. Torn by grief, Tadahiro turned to women and drink to forget his troubles.

To correct his son's dissolute ways Tadamasa turned to his

trusted strongman Umanosuke. Eager to please his lord, Umanosuke placed Tadahiro under house arrest and subjected him to an exceedingly harsh regime of austerity and intense martial practice. It was too much for the effeminate nobleman. Before long he fell ill and after a short sickbed, he died at the age of twenty-nine. Tadahiro's death spelled the end of Umanosuke's career as a Mori retainer. Robbed of his rank he was banished from the Tsuyama fiefdom, never to return again.

Over the next decade, Umanosuke traveled the western provinces in *musha shugyō*. It was probably during this period in his life that Umanosuke visited Musashi in **Kokura**. The *Bushū denraiki* describes how, one day, Umanosuke visited Musashi and challenged him to a friendly match:

武州、大太刀を逆手に持、右馬允が打所を入込て、面を強くひしぐ。ひしがれて身のゝる所を、身をかけて、大指を以て胸をばぐつと突て、あをのけに突倒す。右馬允恐怖し、見物の面々肝膽を作る。

Holding his large tachi in a backhand grip Musashi stooped and struck Umanosuke in the face as he lunged toward him. Umanosuke was thrown back by the impact, but before he knew it Musashi was upon him, thrusting his thumb in Umanosuke's solar plexus and causing him to fall over backward. Umanosuke was terrified and the onlookers were dumbfounded.

Little is known about Umanosuke's later whereabouts. His art of grappling went on to achieve recognition and became widely practiced in the domains of Himeji and Akō. This suggests that, later in life, Omanosuke entered the service of either Matsudaira Tadaakira, the new lord of Himeji castle (who succeeded Honda Masakatsu in 1639), or Asano Naganao, the lord of Akō castle.

Shiota Hamanosuke Kiyokatsu

Shiota Hamanosuke makes several appearances, both in the *Bushū denraiki* and the *Bukōden*. The *Bukōden* describes how, not long after Musashi had joined his son in Kokura:

一打撃て見度願に付、なる程相手になるべしとて、立合けれども、濱之助一向木刀打出事かなわず。捕手も、武公座したもう一間より内に、足を踏入たらば武公の負たるべしとありければ、濱之助大に怒て業をなせども、一間より内に一寸も入事ならず。濱之助、太甚感稱して、武公の門弟となれり。

[Hamanosuke] challenged the swordsman to a bout and, of course, Musashi willingly complied. But Hamanosuke was utterly unable to touch Musashi with his bokutō. And when he resorted to his hoshu jutsu, Musashi simply sat down, telling him that he would floor him if he came within reach. This greatly angered Hamanosuke, who tried a technique on Musashi, but he was unable to come within reach of the swordsman without getting the worst of it. At this Hamanosuke expressed his admiration, and it was from then on that he became one of Musashi's deshi.

Though a native of Harima, Hamanosuke had probably already entered the service of Hosokawa Tadatoshi in Kumamoto by the time he visited Musashi in Kokura. According to the *Bushū denraiki* Musashi requited Hamanosuke's visit by seeking him out in Higo:

或時、肥後へ下向、濱之丞が宅へ旅宿せらる。其頃の諺に、「公方様か、柳生殿か、越中殿か」と申程の兵法者也。近仕の士に、打太刀の者三人有しとかや。越中守殿、三人の輩に、「兵法天下無双、新免武蔵守と云者、塩田濱之丞ガ家に旅宿スといへ。其方共は存たりや」と被尋。三人言葉を揃へ、「御機嫌を見合、是より可申上と存候折柄、御尋被成。御意の如く、濱之丞が宅え罷有よしに候。相越、兵法所望仕度」旨申上る。越中殿被聞召、「一段、尤の事也。早々相越、兵法をも試候へ」と也。

On one occasion Musashi had gone down to Higo and stayed at the house of Hamanosuke. Now Lord Tadatoshi was a heihōsha of such standing that a proverb of the time stated: "Either the shōgun, Lord Yagyū, or Lord Tadatoshi." Among the close retainers of the Hosokawa clan were three practitioners of the art of fighting with the tachi. Speaking to them Lord Tadatoshi said: "I hear that Musashi, the Heihōsha Without Equal Under the Heavens, is staying at the house of Shiota Hamanosuke, did you know this?" His retainers spoke as if with one voice and said: "We were just going to raise the point when you mentioned it. As you say, Musashi is presently staying at the house of Hamanosuke. We intend to go there and test his skills in the art of heihō." Hearing this Lord Tadatoshi said: "This is a good thing. Go there immediately and test your martial skills."

Hosokawa Tadatoshi's Retainers

It was during one of his stays at Shiota Hamanosuke's *yashiki* (see above) that Musashi was visited by three of **Hosokawa Tadatoshi**'s retainers to test Musashi's skill with the sword. They were all practitioners of the Yagyū Shinkage-*ryū*.

The *Bushū denraiki* describes how, after a fair amount of dilly-dallying on the part of the three retainers:

武州早速出られ、「御遠慮に不及儀、早々御立合候へ」と申て、常の木刀二刀にて出合る。板縁のわれたる所に大太刀の先を差入れ、ひらひらと太刀を左右に押たはめ、待居玉ふ。

Musashi came out with his two bokutō and said: "There is no need to stand on ceremony. Let us have a session right now." And as they prepared themselves he thrust the tip of his long bokutō into a gap in the veranda's boards and waited for them, turning and twisting the weapon in the creaking floorboards.

It goes on to describe how:

三人の内、就中巧者の人、庭へをり立。某甚之允と
かや申す［三人の姓名聞候へ共、忘之］。武州も庭
上へをり立、太刀を上段に構、静かなる位にて懸ら
る。甚之允も木刀を前に構てかゝり来る。武州上段
より直に頭に打込るゝ。頭に當りたるかと見へしが
、月代の際にて打留む。甚之允、尻居に打すへらる
。二度目には、武州上段を廣く大きに構、流水の打
にて横より足をなぐらる。木刀を越て、ちうにかや
る。武州二足三足しさらるゝ所を、甚之允ふっと起
あがり、直に打込む。武州入込て、身の當りにて當
らる。二三間はけのきて、のしけに倒れ息絶たり。
漸にして蘇る。

The most talented of the three retainers went and stood in the garden. He was called Jinnosuke, or something (I have heard his surname mentioned but fear I have since forgotten). Musashi, too, went and stood in the garden and approached the man quietly, raising the long I above his head in a jōdan no kamae. Jinnosuke drew near, holding his bokutō in front of him. Then Musashi brought down the weapon on his opponent's head in a straight line. It seemed as if the weapon had struck, but Jinnosuke had stopped it in its track, a hair's breadth above his head. Repelled by the impact, Jinnosuke was thrown to the ground. Next Musashi raised his weapon high and wide and struck out at Jinnosuke's legs with a ryūsui no uchi. But Jinnosuke leapt in the air and let the bokutō pass under him. Musashi now retreated two or three steps, when Jinnosuke suddenly opened the attack and came straight toward him. Musashi, however, ducked and struck Jinnosuke full in the body, causing him to fly through the air and land on his back a few yards away and pass out. At length, he regained consciousness.

* *The ryūsui no uchi, or the "flowing water blow," is also featured in the Water Scroll (Sui no maki) of Musashi's Gorin no sho: "When the opponent retreats quickly, dodges quickly, and quickly parries your tachi, make yourself big, both physically*

and mentally, draw your sword way back behind your body and strike a large and strong blow, but slowly, almost as if there were a stagnation in its motion like one might observe in the rush of a river that tends to flow slower—but with much more force—as it reaches deeper parts."

Intimidated, the remaining two retainers refused to engage in a match with Musashi, acknowledging that Jinnosuke was the most skilled among them.

Ujii Yashirō Mitsunari

Ujii (formerly Urinnin) Yashirō Mitsunari (1581–1669) studied the Shintō-*ryū* under his father, but at a young age took an interest in the **Yagyū Shinkage-ryū**, which he practiced under Yagyū Muneyoshi's star *deshi*, Murata Yazō. He became such a good representative of the Yagyū Shinkage-*ryū* that he was regularly dispatched to *daimyō* who patronized the school, among them Matsudaira Tadaakira (1583–1644), the lord of Kōriyama castle, in the province of Yamato, and Hosokawa Tadatoshi when he still had his headquarters in Kokura castle.

Following Tadatoshi's move to Kumamoto, Yashirō seems to have stayed on in Kokura and temporarily become an instructor in the service of its new lord, Ogasawara Tadazane (1596–1667). However, in the spring of 1633 (well before Musashi joined his son, Iori, in Kokura), Yashirō moved to Kumamoto, where three years later, he became a private fencing instructor to Tadatoshi's retired father, Tadaoki, who was by then residing in Yatsushiro castle, some twenty miles south along the coast from Kumamoto.

It was the lackluster performance of his retainers at Shiota Hamanosuke's *yashiki* that impelled Hosokawa Tadatoshi to call in the help of Yashirō in a final test of Musashi's superiority in the art of swordsmanship.

The *Bukōden* describes how:

時に武公、小倉より召に應じて肥後に来。忠利公懇
望にて、武公と弥四良と御前に於て勝負を決しむ。

One day, in response to a summons from Lord Tadatoshi, Musashi left Kokura and went down to Higo, for it was his lordship's wish that Musashi and Yashirō have a match in his presence.

According to the same record:

武公弥四郎と太刀を持て立合の事、三度に及と雖、
一向弥四良より打出事不叶。武公も御前故、只敵の
技を押へて強く打事なし。

Musashi had three bouts with Yashirō, brandishing his tachi, but not once was Yashirō able to break through his defense. Given that they were fighting in his lordship's presence, Musashi, on his side, satisfied himself with merely countering Yashirō's attacks, without ever striking out forcefully.

It was Yashirō's defeat, finally, that drove Hosokawa Tadatoshi to persuade Musashi to come to Kumamoto and teach the Niten Ichi school as the new school of swordsmanship of the Hosokawa clan.

* *Yashirō had a proud pedigree. His father was Unrinin Dewa no Kami Mitsuhide, who had been a fencing instructor to none other than Oda Nobunaga (1534–82). Mitsuhide had practiced the Shintō school of swordsmanship under Tsukahara Bokuden and taught it to Hikida Bungorō, the favorite pupil of the illustrious Kamiizumi Ise no Kami Nobutsuna. Towards the end of the sixteenth century, he had entered the service of Ōtomo Yoshishige, the Bungo warlord who attacked Kitsuki castle and unleashed the battle on the plains of Ishigahi in which Musashi first saw action.*

MUSASHI'S FRIENDS

It is often said that one can tell a man by his friends. In Musashi's case it is no different: their age, their social standing, and their professions—all say something about the man Musashi.

Most of Musashi's benefactors, though they might have had a soft spot for the swordsman and admired his skill with the sword, would not have considered themselves friends of Musashi, simply because of their high position. Of all of Musashi's benefactors, Mizuno Katsunari was probably closest to the swordsman, especially in his younger years, when both men were residing in Edo and probably practiced together on a regular basis. This much is borne out by a copy of the *Heidō kagami*, which is addressed directly to Katsunari (see Musashi's Benefactors).

Nagaoka Okinaga

One of Musashi's oldest and longest friends is undoubtedly **Nagaoka (also Matsui) Okinaga** (1582–1661). Okinaga had first met Musashi during the Battle of Ishigakihara (see Musashi's Battles). Their friendship deepened when, not long afterward, Musashi's father moved to Kitsuki and became fencing instructor to Okinaga's father, Yasuyuki (1550–1612), the lord of Kitsuki castle. According to the *Bukōden* Okinaga had, like his father, been one of Muni's *deshi* and it is almost certain that both he and Musashi practiced under Musashi's father when they were both living in Kitsuki (see Musashi's Duels).

Not surprisingly, it was Okinaga whom Musashi sought out first when, in the summer of 1612, he arrived in the port of Kokura on his way through to seek out his father, who was still living in Kitsuki. Okinaga, by this time, had just succeeded his own father as master of the Kitsuki fief, but also maintained a large *yashiki* in Kokura to attend to his lord, Hosokawa Tadaoki.

It was Okinaga, too, who arranged the duel with Sasaki Kojirō on Musashi's request (see Musashi's Duels).

Okinaga and Musashi met again later in life when Musashi moved to Kumamoto in the province of Higo at the invitation of Hosokawa Tadatoshi. Okinaga, by then, had lost **Kitsuki castle** under the Bakufu's one-castle-per-province edict. Instead he had been granted a fief of thirty thousand *koku* in the Tamana and Gōshi districts, just north of Kumamoto. Throughout Musashi's last years Okinaga looked after his wellbeing, seeing to it that Musashi received a stipend on which he could support himself, as well as a retinue of some seven aides.

As one of Musashi's oldest friends (he would outlive his friend by thirty-seven years) Okinaga was also one of the senior guests at the swordsman's funeral, which was conducted by the chief abbot Daien Oshō at the Taishō temple, the family temple of the Hosokawa clan in Kumamoto (see Musashi's Burial).

Shiota Hamanosuke Kiyokatsu

One of the men who became close friends with Musashi when he was in his fifties was a man by the name of Shiota Hamanosuke Kiyokatsu (1577–1648). Born in the province of Harima, Kiyokatsu grew up in the village of **Shiota**, the place from which his family derived its name. Situated some ten miles north of the town of Himeji, the hamlet of Shiota has disappeared from the maps, but its name is still remembered by the famous Shitoa hot springs, just outside Yumesaki machi.

Hamanosuke's father had served Akamatsu Norifusa, who had his headquarters at Okishio (also Ojio) castle, which graced the summit of Shiroyama hill, just north of Himeji. In 1580, however, the castle was dismantled as part of Toyotomi Hideyoshi's strategy to bring Harima under his control. It's beams and massive stones were used to construct the To no Ichi gate of Himeji castle, at that time Hideyoshi's headquarters. Five years later, Norifusa was ordered to relocate to Katori castle, in the Province of Awa, on the island of Shikoku.

During the last decade of the sixteenth century, Hamanosuke entered the service of Hosokawa Tadaoki, at that time still the master of Miyazu castle, in province of Tango, on Honshu's western shore. It was probably whilst in Tadaoki's service that he became an expert in the art of *hoshu jutsu*, although it is not known under whom he practiced. In 1600, Hamanosuke followed his lord to Kokura.

When, in 1632, Tadaoki's son, Tadatoshi, was promoted to the fiefdom of Kumamoto, Hamanosuke moved to Kumamoto, where he continued to serve both Tadatoshi and his son, **Hosokawa Mitsunao (1690–50)**, as a *shihan* in the art of *hoshu jutsu*. He also commanded a large retinue of samurai, earning a stipend of fifteen *koku*. He is believed to have died in 1648, three years after his friend, at the age of seventy-one.

It was probably after he had moved to Kumamoto with his lord that Hamanosuke visited Kokura and that he had his first friendly bout with Musashi (see Musashi's Bouts). It is not surprising, then, that later, when Musashi himself moved to Kumamoto, both men became good friends. Indeed, like the *Bukōden* (see Musashi's Bouts), the *Bushū denraiki* claims that Hamanosuke was one of Musashi's many *deshi*:

武州門弟に塩田濱之丞と云者あり。仕物、取篭者など、節々いたしたる者也。細川越中守殿に有附、肥後に住居ス。

Among Musashi's deshi there was a man by the name of Shiota Hamanosuke. He had occasionally practiced shimono and torikago. He was a retainer of Lord Hosokawa Ettchū no Kami Tadatoshi and lived in Higo.

It seems that Hamanosuke had a similar disposition as his famous friend (and teacher) and was known for his quick temper. Thus the *Bushū denraiki* describes how:

武州、肥後に於て、鹽田濱之允所にて、手錠を見玉
ひ、「是にては男子の手には不相應なり。京女抔の
やさしき手には相應の器」との玉ふ。濱之允が腹を
立、「唯今迄數十人の手にをろし候へ共、少も危き
事なし」と答。武州、「さらば、予が手にをろし見
よ」との玉ふ。濱之允、即時に武州の腕にはめ、錠
をゝろす。其時、武州、左右の手に力を入、「えい
」と云て一同に捻玉へば、手錠開き、か子折たり。

One day, while staying at the house of Shiota Hamanosuke in Higo, Musashi was shown a pair of manacles and said: "These are not fit for the wrists of a man. These implements are made for tender wrists such as those of women from Kyoto." At this Hamanosuke grew angry, saying "thus far I have put them on dozens of men, and never once have they let me down." Musashi replied and said: "If that is so, then try and put them on me." No sooner had he said this than Hamanosuke had clamped the manacles around Musashi's wrists and turned the key. Musashi now tensed his left and right hand and, uttering a cry, twisted the manacles and broke them open. The iron had been rent apart under the strain.

That Shiota Hamanosue was not only a friend and close confidant of Musashi but also enjoyed the trust of his lord is borne out by the following passage from the *Bushū denraiki*, which describes how, following Musashi's move to Kumamoto:

越中殿、御許容ありて、臺所辺の入用は、塩田濱之
丞取まかなひ、其身は曽而不存。

Lord Tadatoshi granted Shiota Hamanosuke permission to manage Musashi's allowance, so that Musashi himself need not concern himself with such matters.

Sawamura Daigaku Yoshishige

One of the last men to befriend Musashi was **Sawamura Daigakunosuke Yoshishige** (1560–1650). Daigaku was a longstanding Hosokawa retainer, who had joined the clan in 1582. A native of Wakasa, Yoshishige had a military record at least as impressive as that of his friend. At the time of Musashi's birth, he had already fought several battles, claiming the head of an enemy general, a feat for which he received a reward from none other than Toyotomi Hideyoshi in person.

The two warriors probably first met following Musashi's move to Kumamoto. The *Bushū denraiki* describes how:

武州死去の前々日、細川の家臣・沢村大学が、病床見舞いに訪ねてきた。武州は、枕を上げて、「おいで下さってうれしく思います。今生のお別れです」と申される。

Two days before Musashi's death, the Hosokawa retainer Sawamura Daigaku visited Musashi's sickbed to pay his respect. Musashi propped up his pillow and said: "I am glad that you have come to see me, for this is where we will have to part in this life."

Musashi also seems to have been befriended Daigaku's adopted son, Usaemon Tomoyoshi (1605–60). Usaemon's father, who was already eighty when Musashi moved to Kumamoto in 1640, probably did not study under Musashi. But according to the *Dōsui dengen*, Usaemon himself was one of the fiefdom's many retainers who took up practicing the Niten Ichi-*ryū* under Musashi. Usaemon seems to have also met Musashi outside the *dōjō*. On one occasion, according to the *Bukōden*, "Musashi held a gorgeous banquet under the blossoming cherry trees in the company of master Sawamura Usaemon and half of his *deshi*.

The *Bukōden* also claims that, shortly before his death, "Musashi left a sword forged by Ōhara Sanemori to his friend Sawamura Usaemon," and that "Even now the sword is part of the heirloom of the house of Sawamura. Its length is said to be approximately three feet." It is more likely, however, that Musashi left the sword to Daigaku and that Usaemon inherited the heirloom on his father's death five years after Musashi passed away.

* *Ōhara Sanemori was a swordsmith from Hōki and a distant descendant of the famous Ōhara Yasutsuna, who is believed to have been one of Japan's earliest swordsmiths.*

Akiyama Gentei Wanao

One of Musashi's greatest friendships was undoubtedly that with the monk Akiyama Gentei Wanao (1618–73). Wanao was the junior abbot of the **Taishō temple**, the family temple of the Hosokawa clan in Kumamoto, which stood less than a mile upstream on the western bank of the Shirakawa, the river skirting the eastern walls of Kumamoto castle. The two men probably met not long after Musashi had moved to Kumamoto and moved into his *yashiki* on the former grounds of Chiba castle. Situated on the northeastern side of the Kumamoto castle grounds, it would have only been a ten minute walk for the aged swordsman to visit his friend at the Taishō temple. According to the *Bukōden*:

武公、平居閑静いて、毎に泰勝寺の住持春山和尚に参禅し、連歌或は書畫小細工等を仕て、日月を過了す。故に武公作の鞍、楊弓、木刀、連語、書画、数多あり。

Musashi led a peaceful and quiet life at Kumamoto and frequently visited Akiyama Wanao, the chief abbot of the Taishō temple, passing the days in composing renga, practicing calligraphy, and making handicrafts. As a result, there are a great number of sword sheaths, bows, bokutō, renga, and calligraphies from his hand.

Though they were separated by an age gap of thirty-four years, soon a deep spiritual friendship developed between these two so disparate men, a friendship forged in their shared awareness of the fleeting nature of human existence. Like the famous friendship between the great swordsman Yagyū Munenori and the buddhist priest and intellectual Takuan Sōhō, the monk had a lasting influence on Musashi's spiritual and philosophical outlook on life.

The weight Musashi attached to his friendship with Wanao is borne out by his request that the young monk help him with the preface of his life's work: the *Gorin no sho*. According to the *Bukōden*, Wanao complied, although he was careful not to distort the meaning of Musashi's words:

序は龍田山泰勝寺春山和尚［泰勝寺第二世也］に雌黄を乞ふ。春山、これには斧鑿を加ふれ寸は却て其素意を失ん事を愁て、更に文躰法度に不拘、唯文字の差誤せる所までを改換、且つ義理の近似なる古語を引用て潤色之と也。

Musashi asked Akiyama Wanao (the second-generation abbot of the Taishō temple) to correct its preface. Fearful that the text might lose its true meaning through any elaborations, Akiyama refrained from changing the structure of the text in any way, limiting himself to the correction of wrongly written characters and citing old sayings that immediately pertained to the text.

Upon Musashi's death, on 13 June 1645, his burial ceremony at the Taishō temple was conducted by the temple's senior abbot, Daien Ōshō. Yet following the ceremony, according to the *Bukōden*, the coffin was brought to the Maesugi horse grounds of the Taishō temple, where Akiyama Wanao performed the last rites (see Musashi's Burial).

It is also believed that, at the request of Musashi's son, Iori, Wanao drafted the *Kokura hibun*, the lengthy epitaph engraved on the obelisk-like monument erected at Temukeyama near Kokura nine years after Musashi's death. (see Musashi's Places).

MUSASHI'S DESHI

Musashi is said to have thousands of followers during his life-time. The *Dosui dengen*, for instance, claims that during his last years in Higo Musashi had close to a thousand *deshi*.

Musashi's *deshi* included men of high rank such as Matsudaira Katsutaka (1589–1666), friends like Shiota Hamanosuke, down to samurai of low birth, simple foot soldiers in the service of Musashi's benefactors. Here, we will limit ourselves to Musashi's most important *deshi*. It is clear from the records that his most favored students were the Terao brothers, Magonojō Nobumasa (1613–72), and his younger brother by a decade, Motomenosuke Nobuyuki (1621–88).

The Terao Brothers

The Terao brothers came from a proud line of Hosokawa retainers whose ancestry went back to the Nitta, the clan that had brought forth the great **Nitta Yoshisada** (1301–38), the hero of the Two Courts period (1333–92). Their distant ancestor, Terao Magoshirō, had been the master of Takano castle, in the province of Kai.

Kai, at the time, was ruled by the powerful **Takeda Shingen** (1521–73). Magoshirō, who had entered Shingen's service at the age of sixteen, proved a great warrior, distinguishing himself on the field of battle and receiving Takano castle and its domain in reward.

During the seventies, following Shingen's death and the loss of their castle, Magoshirō moved westward, toward the province of Bizen, where he became enfeoffed to the warlord Ukita Naoie (1529–1582), and settled in Sawada, one mile east of the warlord's headquarters of Okayama castle.

When, in the summer of 1600, Naoie's son, **Ukita Hideie** (1572–1655), rallied his clansmen to do battle against Ieyasu's eastern forces at Sekigahara, the Terao clan was led by Magoshirō's son, who was named after his father. It is believed the latter died on the plains of Sekigahara, but his son, Sasuke Katsunaga survived.

Following the demise of the Ukita clan, Katsunaga, had (like Muni's lord, Shinmen Munetsura) moved to the southern island of Kyushu. Katsunaga entered the service of **Hosokawa Tadaoki** (1563–1646), who had by then been promoted to the Kokura fiefdom in reward for his services in the same battle. By the time Hosokawa Tadaoki passed the reins on to his son, Tadatoshi, Terao Katsunaga was in command of a contingent of fifty *teppō ashigaru* and a fief with a yield of one thousand *koku*. By then he had sired five sons, the eldest of whom was Kurōzaemon Katsumasa.

* *It will be noted that, unlike Terao Katsumasa and Shinmen Munetsura, Musashi's father, Muni, already moved down to Kyushu before the Battle of Sekigahara (see Musashi's Father).*

Terao Magonojō Masanobu

Terao Magonojō Nobumasa was Katsunaga's second son. He was small in stature and partly deaf, and it is believed that he spent some time on the road as a *rōnin*. During the Shimabara Rebellion (1638), however, he answered his clan's rallying cry and joined his brothers in battle. In 1640, upon Tadatoshi's promotion to the fiefdom of Kumamoto, he moved to Higo, but like his great mentor, Musashi, he refused to enter his lordship's service. Instead, he seems to have supported himself by working a small plot of land and (especially after Musashi's death) teaching Musashi's Niten Ichi-*ryū*.

It is not clear at what stage Nobumasa and his younger brother, Nobuyuki, first met Musashi, but the most plausible scenario is that they became his pupils after Musashi moved down from Akashi to Kokura upon **Ogasawara Tadazane**'s promotion to the eponymous fiefdom in 1632. Both brothers, after all, were born in Kokura and the *Bushū denraiki* clearly states that Nobumasa inherited the teachings of Musashi's Niten Ichi-*ryū* "through diligent practice over many years"—something that could not have been the case had he only studied under the swordsman during his last five years in Kumamoto.

* *Nobumasa and his brother may even have visited Musashi at Akashi prior to 1632, for his uncle, Terao Sakuzaemon, had not moved to Kyushu in the wake of the Battle of Sekigahara, but entered the service of Honda Tadamasa, the daimyō of Himeji and one of Musashi's many benefactors. It is more than probable that Sakuzaemon was among one of Musashi's many* deshi *in Himeji before the latter moved to Akashi.*

It seems that, in spite of his independence, Nobumasa led a good life. In a special appendix, Tanji Hōkin, the author of the *Bushū denraiki*, claims that:

熊本の城下近邑に引籠り、耕して生涯を送り、福力あつて米銭に乏しからずと云り。武州公数百人の門人より撰出し傳授ありし人也。法名夢世と號す。小兵ながら力量有しと云り。寺尾の本家、今尚細川の家臣たり。

Nobumasa lived in rural retreat near the castle of Kumamoto, where he spent his life cultivating a small plot of land. He had the power of wealth, never being in need of neither rice nor money. Nobumasa was selected by Musashi from among several hundred men and initiated in the Niten Ichi art of heihō. His Buddhist name was Muyo, and though he was of small stature he was a man of great strength. Even today the members of the head clan to which Terao belonged serve as retainers to the house of Hosokawa.

In old age Nobumasa moved down to Uto, settling in Matsuyama and remaining there until his death, on 8 November 1672 at the age of fifty-nine.

For a long time **Nobumasa's grave** was lost, probably by successive earthquakes or during extensive allied bombing during the Second World War. But in the summer of 1993 local historian, Nagai Kaiichrō (1920–1995) rediscovered the damaged gravestone among the trees on Goshiki Hill, in the city's Matsuyama township. An expert on local history, Nagai had Nobumasa'sgrave restored and re-erected on a graveyard on the hills western slope, at the location where the stones were found.

Terao Motomenosuke Nobuyuki

Unlike his older brother, Terao Motomenosuke Nobuyuki, who was Katsunaga's third son, entered the service of the Hosokawa clan like his remaining brothers. He did so in 1633 as a page to his lordship at the age of thirteen. Three years later, when he went through the *genpuku* ceremony and reached adulthood, he was a regular retainer on a stipend of two hundred *koku*. Standing almost six feet tall, he cut an impressive figure, especially when compared to his older brother. He was a formidable warrior and was rewarded for his display of bravery in the suppression of the Shimabara Rebellion. By the time Nobuyuki reached his forties, he was in command of twenty *teppō ashigaru* on a stipend of three hundred *koku*.

Following Musashi's death, Nobuyuki moved to the Uto district, where he held fiefs in Hachikubo and Matsuyama (today both located in the city of Uto), some five miles south of Kumamoto.

Nobuyuki's grave lies at Nishi no Musashizuka, or the western Musashi burial mound, situated in Kumamoto's western Shimasaki ward. Close by stands a withered rock flanked by two lanterns. Engraved with the inscription *Shingen Koji*, or "Buddhist layman Shingen," it marks the place where some believe Musashi's remains rest until this day (see Musashi's Grave). In fact, it is probably the grave of one of Nobuyuki's descendants who, out of devotion for the founding father of their school of swordsmanship, also took on the name of Shingen. Thus, Nobuyuki's fourth son, Nobumori, is known to have taken on the spiritual name of Shinmen Bennosuke (新免弁助) in reverence for his father's teacher.

The Inheritors of Musashi's Legacy

It seems that in Musashi's eyes, at least, both brothers were on equal footing, for the *Bukōden* adds that both:

兄弟は、武公親睦して、常に細工等をして、諸弟の
稽古にも交らず、終に一流相傳なり。

The brothers were on intimate terms with Musashi and would often work with him on tactics, without joining the other deshi in practice. Eventually, the two brothers became the sole progenitors of the Niten Ichi school of swordsmanship.

Being the sole progenitors of the Niten Ichi school of swordsmanship, it was to the two Terao brothers, therefore, that Musashi entrusted his writings (see Musashi's Writings). Being the eldest of the two brothers, it was to Nobumasa that, according to the *Bukōden*:

正保二年五月十二日、五輪書を寺尾孫之亟勝信 ［後
剃髪、夢世云］に相傳在。三十九ヶ條の書を寺尾求
馬信行に相傳なり。

On 12 May of the second year of Shōhō [6 June 1645], Musashi handed the Gorin no sho to Terao Magonojō Nobumasa (who afterward took the tonsure and took on the name of Muse). The Heihō sanjū-kyū kajō he handed to Terao Motomenosuke Nobuyuki.

MUSASHI'S WEAPONS

As a warrior who had made his living by the sword, Musashi had a large collection of weapons, chief among them a collection of prized swords he accumulated in the course of his martial career that spanned almost half a century.

Musashi's Swords

One of the swords in Musashi's possession, according to the *Bukōden* was a three feet long sword made by Ōhara Sanemori, a swordsmith from Hōki and a descendant of Ōhara Yasutsuna, one of Japan's earliest swordsmiths, who was active during the Heian period. Another sword, a two feet and eight inches long *tachi*, was forged by Takada Masayuki, a well-known swordsmith from Bungo. Given that both smiths were active during Musashi's lifetime, it is highly probable that Musashi had his swords tailor-made. True to his disdain for ostentation, according to the *Bukōden*:

武公大小刀の拵えは、總て金飾へを不用、脇差には
金飾あり。刀は、他所にて廣間などの手遠き所にも
置物なれば、若金など迦む事あり、さあれば、不覚
悟に見ゆるなり。脇差は身を放ず物なれば、其心じ
かいなしと也。

None of Musashi's swords, long or short, were finished with gold, although his wakizashi was. Swords, after all, might be put aside when visiting someone's place, and to have one's weapons inlaid with gold might give people the impressions that they were merely ornamental and their owner not prepared for the worst. His wakizashi, however, would never leave his belt, so it did not matter if it were ornamented with gold.

The most prized piece among Musashi's sword collection was a sword that had been given to him by Hosokawa Tadatoshi, the benefactor on whose invitation he had spent his last years at Kumamoto. The same record describes that its ornaments were made of solid gold, and that:

新しく一腰掛の刀掛を造り、餘の道具を不掛、拝領
の刀までを掛けて、常に床の上に置れしとゆ。

As it was an ornamental sword, Musashi attached to it a new cord to suspend it from the waist of his armor, something he did not do with any of his other swords. It always took pride of place in the alcove of his house.

According to anecdote, Musashi was an aficionado of the swords made by Kamiizumi Kaneshige, a *tōkō* (刀工), or sword-smith, from a long line of artisan smiths from Seki going all the way back to Kamiizumi Kanesada, whose earliest extant work is dated the second month of Kyōtoku (February 1455). Starting out as a maker of arrowheads, or *yajiri* (鏃), Kaneshige quickly became one of Edo's foremost sword-smiths and is said to have become a house artisan to Todō Takatora (1556–1630), the *daimyō* of the Imabarai fiefdom in the province of Iyo on Musashi's recommendation.

The chroniclers recorded how the master left many of his swords to his disciples and friends. The *Bukōden*, for instance, describes how:

高田貞行作の刀、長さ二尺八寸あるを岡部九左右衛
門所持せり。裏に新免武藏守と銘あり。故嘉太夫時
、壽之主被召上、後に道家平藏に賜ふ。平藏は、武
公の直弟寺尾求馬の門弟にて、兵法一流相傳あり。

The sword forged by Takada Masayuki is two feet and eight inches long and is now in the possession of Okabe Kyūsaemon. Under the hilt, it has the inscription "Shinmen Musashi no Kami." During the times of [Okabe] Kadayū it was confiscated by Nagaoka Hisayuki, who passed it on to Dōke Heizō, who studied the Niten Ichi-ryū under one of Musashi's direct pupils, Terao Motomenosuke.

Sadly, none of the swords described have ever been found. The Yatsushiro Municipal Museum still has a sword among its vast collection that stems from the collection of the Terao clan, but unlike the sword described in the *Bukōden*, it does not carry an inscription on its tang by which it can be traced to Musashi. The Shimada Museum of Art in Kumamoto has among its vast collection of medieval swords two swords ascribed to Musashi. One is a sword without a swordsmith's signature (*mei*) dating back to the Nanobukuchō period (1336–92). The other is a Muromachi period (1333–1568) sword carrying the signature of Kunimune.

Musashi's Bokutō

It is perhaps not surprising that, perhaps with the exception of the oar with which he defeated Sasaki Kojirō on Funashima Island, not one of Musashi's *bokutō* has survived (see Reigan Cave). Tough made of highly endurable Japanese hardwoods, *bokutō* were merely a tool for practice; not a symbol of status, let alone a relic to be cherished and handed down from generation to generation. What makes this all the more regrettable is that many of Musashi's hardwood weapons were crafted by the master swordsman himself. The *Bukōden* describes how, during the last years of his life in Kumamoto:

武公、平居閑静して、毎に泰勝寺の住持春山和尚に
参禅し、連歌或は書畫小細え等を仕て、日月を過了
す。故に武公作の鞍・楊弓・木刀・連歌・書画、數
多あり。

Musashi led a peaceful and quiet life and frequently visited Akiyama Wanao, the abbot of the Taishō temple. He passed the days in composing renga, practicing calligraphy, and making handicrafts. As a result, there are a great number of sword sheaths, bows, bokutō, renga, and calligraphies from his hand.

Being an expression of the swordsman's creative genius as well as a relic, some of Musashi's *bokutō* did survive their owner, albeit not to this day. Thus the *Tōsakushi* mentions that one of Musashi's *bokutō* was in the possession of a certain Moriiwa Nagataifu:

長さ三尺六寸五分、厚み一方は四分五厘、一方は二
歩五厘。正中に稜あり、此所にて厚さ五分、上下と
も端圓くして首尾相同じ。枇杷の木なり［色黒く大
に煤付て古びたり］。

Its length is three feet and six shaku, four bu, and five ri [approx. three-and-a-half feet], its thickness on one side is four bu and five rin [approx. half and inch], and on the other side two bu and five rin [approx. a quarter of an inch]. Along its center runs an edge, at which place it is five bu thick, and its upper and lower edge is rounded all the way through. It is made of a loquat tree (its color being black and having an exceedingly old and stained look).

* *Over the centuries, the size of the* shaku *has differed, even from region to region, giving rise to different names, such as the kanejaku, the kujirajaku, and the gofukujaku. During the Meiji period (1868–1912), however, the shaku was standardized, in that the kanejaku was adopted as the national unit of measurement at 33.303 cm, or just under one foot. Unlike the foot, the shaku is divided into ten units instead of twelve to arrive at the Japanese equivalent of the inch, which is called a* sun. *The* sun, *in turn, is divided into ten* bu.

Nothing is known about Moriiwa Nagataifu, but the *Tōsakushi* mentions that a certain Moriiwa Hikobei (probably one of Nagataifū's ancestors) lived in Miyamoto and claims that "he would accompany Miyamoto Musashi to the Kamazaka hills of Nakamura whenever he went on one of his *musha shugyō*." It is not impossible that Musashi gave one of his *bokutō* to Hikobei as an expression of gratitude and that the weapon was passed down the generations until, somewhere during the early nineteenth century, it was inherited by Nagataifū.

MUSASHI'S INJURIES

Going by the records, Musashi was wounded only three times in his long career as a warrior, none of them life-threatening. His first taste of the dangers of combat came at the early age of sixteen when he was struck in the waist by a *yari* while taking part in the siege of Tomiku castle alongside the forces of Kuroda Yoshitaka in 1600 (See Musashi's Battles). The *Bushū denraiki* describes how:

馬糞を取て疵口にをし入れ、少も痛ム面色なく、城
へ乗上り能働き、其後小屋へ歸ても、朋友の手負を
見廻に、杖にすがりて、痛める色なく徘徊せられし
と云り。

He simply took some horse dung, pushed it into the wound and, without a trace of pain on his face, climbed back toward the castle and continued to fight. Afterward, when they had returned to the camp, it is said that he went round to visit the wounded, leaning on a staff, and loitering about without any signs of being in pain.

For twelve years Musashi seems to have remained unharmed. This is truly remarkable, given that he is said to have participated in no less than sixty duels during this time in his life. He might have sustained minor cuts and bruises, but the first next recorded injury was in his duel with Sasaki Kojirō on Funashima island (see Musashi's Duels). The *Bushū denraiki* describes how, in the course of that duel, Kojirō's grip on his longsword slipped, and the blade struck Musashi flat on the neck. It goes on to describe how, on the point of leaving Funashima island in Muraya Kanpachirō's boat:

初めカルサンを切らせたる事は、諸人見及故、高く
かゝげ、平首にあたりたるは、はげしき場ゆへ見届
けたる者なし。太刀が平打ながら、したゝかに打た
るにより、血も少は流れしを、下着の襟を出し、疵
を隠されたりとかや。

Musashi held his karusan (hakama) aloft to show to the gathered crowd that it was cut, but in the fierceness of the encounter no one had seen that he had been hit in the neck. And while it had only been the flat side of Kojirō's blade, due to the force of the blow, blood was oozing out of the wound so that Musashi pulled up the collar of his undergarment to hide the wound.

Though the wound was not life-threatening it was serious enough for Musashi to take refuge at Moji castle in the wake of the duel, although, according to the *Numata kaki*, it was chiefly to escape Kojirō's many followers and wait until the dust had settled.

Musashi's sustained his last battle injury during the suppression of the Shimabara Rebellion. At Lord Ogasawara Tadazane's request, he was assigned to an escort to protect the lord's son, Ogasawara Nagatsugu (1615–66). The *Bushū denraiki* describes how:

城乗の時、賊徒石を抛つ。馬前に来る石を、「石がまいる」と言葉をかて、五尺杖にてつき戻し。

During the storming of the castle the rebels threw down stones, but Musashi leapt in front of the horse and, shouting "beware of the stones," he fended them off with his staff.

Though it does not mention that Musashi was injured, a letter from Musashi to Arima Naozumi (1586–1641) confirms that Musashi "was struck on the shins twice by rocks, making it impossible for me to put any weight on my legs at present." These injuries, combined with his failing health, were probably the reason why Musashi also refrained from fighting any duels. The last time he took up a weapon was when, on Lord Hosokawa Tadatoshi's request, he agreed to engage in a friendly match with the Yagyū Shinkage-*ryu* adept, Ujii (formerly Urinnin) Yashirō Mitsunari (1581–1669), on the grounds of Kumamoto castle.

MUSASHI'S DEATH

It is clear now that already during his stay in Kokura with his son following Ogasawara Tadazane's promotion in 1632, Musashi increasingly began to suffer from some sort of affliction of the throat. This is first revealed in a letter he wrote to Hosokawa Tadatoshi's Head of Pages, Sakazaki Naizen, after he had been approached to come and stay in Kumamoto (see Musashi's Benefactors). In the letter, Musashi reveals that he has chosen to write because he could "not reply orally" to Naizen's messenger, Iwama Rokubei Masanari.

Musashi did not reveal what affliction exactly he was suffering from. Yet given the symptoms, it was most likely dyspagia, which affects the food pipe and can be caused by cancer. That Musashi's affliction had developed into full-blown throat cancer by the time he had moved to Kumamoto is borne out by the *Bushū denraiki*, which claims that Musashi "was taken ill with esophageal cancer (*ekkaku*), before he found the time to write out a fair copy" of his life's work, the *Gorin no sho*.

From the correspondence between Iori and Tadatoshi's senior retainer, Nagaoka Kenmotsu, it is now clear that, by the end of 1644, Musashi's condition had deteriorated to such an extent that he was no longer able to teach his many students in Kumamoto. Yet, despite the cold of winter, he did continue to visit the Reigan Cave to work on his *Gorin no sho*. Writing to Iori on 17 December, Kenmotsu explains how:

熊本へお出でいただき養生したほうが良しと、佐渡守と私から申し使わしましたが、同心されませんでした。しかしながら、藩主光尚もことのほか念頃に申され、医者などもたびたび派遣され、色々と養生させられて、やはり在郷にては養生の指図も難しき、度々出てこられる様に申されましたので、一作日熊本へ出てこられました。其所で養生をさらにお世話を致し、油断なく指図致しますし、藩主光尚も念頃に思い医者なども付け置かれた。

Master Nagaoka Okinaga and I implored him to come down to Kumamoto so that we could nurse him there, yet he would not comply. Lord Mitsunao, too, kindly urged him to do so and frequently dispatched a physician, nursing him in various ways. But since it was difficult to conduct such care where he was staying, he was urged to regularly come to Kumamoto, so that, the day before yesterday, he finally came down to Kumamoto. There, we increased his care, never letting up our guard in our directions to his servants, including Lord Mitsunao, who appointed a physician to be at his side constantly.

* *Born as Komeda Yoshichirō, Kenmotsu (1586–1658) was the eldest son of Komeda Koremasa, a retainer in the service of Hosokawa Tadaoki. In 1607, following a dispute with a senior retainer, Kenmotsu left the service of the Hosokawa and subsequently joined the ranks of Toyotomi Hideyori's troops during the siege of Osaka castle. In 1623 he returned to Kumamoto and re-entered Tadatoshi's service on a stipend of two thousand koku, upon which he received the name Nagaoka Kenmotsu. Over the following years, Kenmotsu steadily climbed in rank until, in 1634, he reached the position of senior retainer with a fief of ten thousand koku.*

For the next six months, Musashi remained at his *yashiki* in Kumamoto, continuing to work on his *Gorin no sho* while being nursed by a physician. The *Bukōden* records how, "on 13 June 1645 Musashi passed away in his house at [the former site of] Chiba castle in Kumamoto," while the *Heihō senshi denki* describes in reverend detail how, at the final moment of his death:

帯をしめ、脇差しを帯し、片膝を立て、刀を左に杖に突きて終わられけるとぞ。

Musashi had his belt tightened, and his wakizashi inserted into his belt. Then he sat there kneeling on the floor with one knee raised, leaning on his katana with his left hand, until his spirit departed from earth.

MUSASHI'S BURIAL

According to his son, Iori's, correspondence, Musashi's burial ceremony was conducted by Daien Oshō. Oshō was the first abbot of the **Taishō temple**, which stood less than a mile upstream on the western bank of the Shira-*kawa*, the river skirting the eastern walls of Kumamoto castle. According to the *Bukōden*, however, an important role is ascribed to Akiyama Wanao (1618–73). Wanao was the second abbot of the Taishō temple, and is believed to have befriended Musashi during his last years in Kumamoto (see Musashi's Friends):

卒去の時、遺言の通り、甲冑を帯し六具を固めて入
棺であった。飽田郡小江村の地に埋葬した。かねて
の約束で、泰勝寺の前杉馬場の内に棺を舁ぎ据え、
春山和尚が出迎えて、引導した。これはみな遺言に
よってのことである。

On his death, Musashi was laid in his coffin in full armor with all his weapons, as he had requested. He was buried in the village of Oe in the Akita district. As was previously arranged, the coffin was brought to the Maesugi horse grounds of the Taishō temple, where Akiyama Wanao performed the last rites.

The Maesugi horse grounds were at the southern entrance to Taishō temple compound. It was there that the procession was brought to a halt, that Musashi's coffin was placed on a large rock along the right side of the road leading down to the river, and that Akiyama Wanao said a requiem for his departed friend. The rain season had started and it was pouring down with rain, and it is said that no sooner had Wanao performed the last rites than a massive bolt of lightning lit up the grey sky. Today, the Maesugi horse grounds have been swallowed up by Kumamoto's urban sprawl, but the stone, marked by a pylon, is still in situ.

GLOSSARY

ashigaru: — Foot soldier.

bokken: — Wooden practicing sword.

bokutō: — Wooden sword used for practice.

bun-bu: — Used to refer to a warrior's civil and martial accomplishments.

daimyō: — Feudal lord.

denki: — Biography.

deshi: — Pupil or desciple of a master of an art or craft who had committed himself or herself to study the art or craft in question for a number of years.

dōjō: — Hall with a smooth wooden floor or covered with mats for the practice of martial arts.

hakama: — Trousered skirt, worn by the samurai.

haori: — Lightweight silk jacket originally meant to be worn by men as a component of the *hakama*.

heihō: — Art or method of warfare, here generally employed to mean the martial arts, and in particular Musashi's Niten Ichi-*ryū*.

heihōsha: — Practitioner of the art of *heihō*.

hoshu jutsu: — Compendium of seizing, holding, and binding techniques employed to arrest culprits or deal with those who had been captured alive during siege warfare.

jitte: — A traditional weapon consisting of an iron rod that may vary in length between thirty centimeters to a meter with a fork-like extension situated just above the hilt.

jūjutsu: — Bare-handed form of combat art based on a variety of grappling techniques.

kaishaku: — The person whose role it was to behead the one committing *seppuku*. Usually, the *kaishaku* was a confidant of the person committing *seppuku*.

karusan hakama: — *Hakama* with trouser legs that tapered toward the lower end so that they sat tight round the lower shins.

koku:	Medieval unit of measurement, approximately 180 liters. Here it is used to express the annual rice yield of a plot of land, one *koku* being sufficient to keep a man alive for a year.
musha bugyō:	Magistrate of Warriors.
musha shugyō:	Literally, "warrior training" but in the context of *budō*, the old practice of ascetic self-discipline that goes back to the ancient traditions of the so-called *yamabushi*, or enigmatic mountain monks.
naginata:	Pole sword.
omoimono:	Classical Japanese term that can mean either a loved one or a prostitute.
rōnin:	Masterless samurai.
renga:	Series of short verses that are linked into one single poem through a collaborative effort.
ryūha:	A particular branch of a school of fencing.
seppuku:	Ritual suicide.
shaku:	Measure of length, about one foot.
shiai:	Contest between two martial artists.
shihan:	Chief instructor.
shinken:	Real sword.
shoshidai:	Head of the Samurai Dokoro.
shōgun:	Hereditary military governor during Japan's fuedal era.
tachi:	Longest of the pair of swords traditionally worn by samurai.
tantō:	Short dagger.
teppō ashigaru:	An *ashigaru* (foot soldiers) armed with a musket (*teppō*).
uchidachi:	The senior sparring partner when practicing *kata*. The junior sparring partner is called *shidachi*.
wakizashi:	Shortest of the pair of swords traditionally worn by samurai.
yari:	Spear or lance.
yashiki:	Medieval nobleman's mansion.
zōei bugyō:	Construction Magistrate.

INDEX

A

Akamatsu Mochisada 20
Akamatsu Norifusa 142
Akashi castle 21, 54–55, 87–88,
    131
Akiyama Gentai Wanao 19, 28,
    103–104, 146–48, 157, 163
Akizuki castle 3
Akō castle 135
Amago Haruhisa 8, 11–12
Amago Katsuhisa 13
Amakusa Shiro 45
Andō Naotsugu 133
Arima Kihei 67, 105, 120
Arima Naozumi 46, 96, 160
Asano Naganao 135
Ashikaga Yoshiaki 107
Ashikaga Yoshiharu 107
Ashikaga Yoshiteru 107

B

Bessho Nagaharu 13–14, 20–21
Bessho Shigeharu 21, 67
Bingo Go-kuni shrine 43, 58, 91
Bisan hōkan 53, 87, 121–22
Bukōden 10, 20–21, 28–30, 49,
    60–61, 73–76, 97–98,
    100–118, 136, 140—48,
    152, 155–57, 162–63
Bushū denraiki 15, 18, 22,
    25–29, 33–34,37–38, 46,
    51–52, 54, 58–60, 69,
    73–75, 77, 93–95, 100,
    105–19, 126–37, 143–45,
    151, 159–61

C

Chiba castle 97–98, 146, 162

D

Daien Oshō 142, 163
Dōbō goen 26
Dōke Kakusaemon 74
Dōmyōji Tenman shrine 82
Dōrin 2, 6, 48, 67, 69

E

Edo castle 77, 92, 126
Engyō temple 17–18
Enmei-*ryū* 30, 86, 90
Ennin 76
Enyū, Emperor 75

F

Fuchida Yagihei 101
Fujiwara Kanehira 89
Fukuyama castle 43, 58, 90, 92
Fushimi castle 49

G

Gan-*ryū* 114, 118
Ganryū Island 60–61, 79, 98
Gekken sōdan 1, 108
Genbō Hideyuki 107
Genkōan monastery 73
Genzaemon Naotsuna 108
Gifu castle 49, 56
Go-Daigo, Emperor 31
Gorin no sho vii, 1, 2, 47, 98,
    104–105, 120, 138, 147,
    161–62
Gotō Mototsugu 41, 82, 83

H

Hachidai shrine 75–77

Hamanosuke 136–37, 139, 142–45, 149
Hara castle 45–46, 57, 95–96, 131
Harima kagami 1, 4, 21, 23, 30, 47, 95
Hassha Jūemon 9
Heidō kagami 30–31, 56, 91, 141
Heihō senshi denki 102, 118, 132, 162
Himeji castle 5, 17–18, 52–53, 86, 121, 135, 143
Hinokuma castle 69
Hinoshita Kaizan Shinmei Miyamoto Musashi Seimei-*ryū* 30
Hirano Yōsai 4–5, 21
Hōgan castle 9
Hōkoku shrine 2
Hōkōsho 16, 24, 35
Honchō bugei shoden 1, 3–4, 7, 30, 110
Honda Masakatsu 135
Honda Masatomo 122
Honda Sakyō 41, 84
Honda Tadamasa 17, 25, 52, 54, 86, 87, 121–22, 151
Honda Tadatoki 17, 19, 24–25, 35, 39
Hontai Yōshin-*ryū* 133
Hosokawa Mitsunao 99, 143
Hosokawa Tadaoki 60–61, 70, 114–16, 139, 141, 143, 150, 162
Hosokawa Tadatoshi 2, 10, 38, 47, 60–61, 69–70, 97, 99, 136–42, 155, 160–61

Hōzō monastery 80–81
Hōzōin Kakuzenbō In'ei 80
Hōzōin-*ryū* 80, 119, 133

I

Ichjō temple 74
Ideta Hidenobu 98
Ikeda Masakoto 16, 25, 35, 44
Ikeda Mitsumasa 25, 122
Ikeda Terumasa 52
Ikeda Toshitaka 52
ikkan Shimizu 66
Iwahara Gyūnosuke 17, 19

K

Kamiizumi Kaneshige 156
Kanemaki Jisai 114
Kasadera Kannon temple 88–89
Katsuhime 25
Kawaradake castle 69
Kawasaki Kaginosuke 87, 120
Keichō nenchū samurai-chū jija chigyō 9
Keichō nikki 10
Kinmei, Kinmei 85
Kinoshita Nobutoshi 10
Kitano Tenman shrine 74
Kitayama Betsu monastery 75
Kitsuki castle 10, 69–70, 115, 140–42
Kiyomizu temple 72
Kojima Yoshishige 132
Kōkai fūhansō 79
Kōkō zatsuroku 38–43, 84, 85
Kokura castle 24, 59–61, 69, 94, 127, 139
Kokura hibun 3–4, 7, 19, 73, 74, 104, 111–18, 148

Kōriyama castle 139
Koro usawa 74, 108–109
Kōshū-*ryū* 1, 64
Kōzuki castle 13
Kumamoto castle 97–99, 102, 146, 160, 163
Kuroda Nagamasa 38, 123, 126, 130
Kuroda Toshitaka 37, 51, 68
Kuroda Yoshitaka 37–38, 48, 51, 69, 97, 159
Kusakari Tarōemon Shigetsugu 7
Kuwana castle 53

M

Masaki Teruo 1, 7, 24, 63, 65, 68
Mataichi Naoshige 108, 110
Matsudaira Katsutaka 58–59, 93–94, 127–28, 149
Matsudaira Kunzan 40, 42
Matsudaira Naomasa 59, 128
Matsudaira Shigekatsu 127
Matsudaira Tadaakira 135, 139
Matsudaira Yasuchika 1, 24, 63
Matsue castle 59, 60, 128
Matsukura Shigehari 44
Matsuyama castle 59–60, 93, 127–28
Mikami Genryū 1
Miki castle 13, 20–21
Mimasaka ryakushi 30
Minagi Yasuzane 9
Miyake Gunbei or Gundayū 120
Miyake Gundayū 53, 87
Miyamot Mikinosuke 15–19, 24, 35, 39, 44, 53–54, 86, 120

Miyamoto Iori 3, 7, 14, 16, 19, 20–25, 30, 35, 46–47, 55, 66, 88, 94–96, 102, 104, 130–31, 139, 148, 161, 163
Miyamoto Kōhei 16, 35, 39, 44
Miyamoto Kurōtarō 24–25
Miyata Kanbei 19
Mizuno Katsunari 16, 38–41, 43, 44–49, 53, 56–58, 77, 82–85, 90–92, 141
Mizuno Katsutoshi 41, 44, 84
Moji castle 60–61, 70, 78–79, 115, 117–18, 160
Mori Tadahiro 134
Mori Tadamasa 134
Moriiwa Nagataifu 157–58
Motomenosuke Nobuyuki 103, 149, 153
Mukashibanashi 89, 93, 125
Murase Saba 41, 84
Musashi Meisō Ishi 43, 58, 91
Musashizuka 103, 153
Musō Gonnosuke Katsuyoshi 123

N

Nagai Kaiichrō 153
Nagaoka Kenmotsu 161, 162
Nagaoka Okinaga 2, 38, 70–71, 114, 141, 162
Nagaoka Yasuyuki 10, 115, 141
Nagaoka Yoriyuki 98
Nagoya castle 89, 92
Nakagawa Shimanosuke 16, 35, 39, 44, 57
Nakagawabara castle 16, 44, 57
Nakamura Ichiemon Naomasa 131

Nakatsu castle 51, 60, 68
Nakayama Fumio 43, 91
Nakayama Kageyu 41–42, 84
Nakayama Shigemori 43, 58, 90–91
Nenami Okuyama Jion 80
Nihon kendō-shi 121, 122
Nihon Shoki 68
Nijō, Emperor 73
Niten Ichi-*ryū* 28, 133, 145, 150–51, 156
Nitenki 74, 75, 81, 114, 118, 125
Nitta Yoshisada 149
Numata kaki 38, 70, 78, 117–18, 160
Numata Nobumoto 78, 117

O

Oba Heiba 43
Oda Nobunaga 13, 114, 129, 140
Ōgaki castle 49, 56
Ogasawara Nagatsugu 46, 97, 160
Ogasawara Tadazane 2, 22, 24, 38, 46, 54–55, 61–62, 87, 94–95, 102, 119, 127, 130–31, 139, 151, 160–61
Ogawa Gondayū Rōshin 129–30
Ōhara Sanemori 146, 155
Ōjin, Emperor 84, 85
Okayama castle 16, 35, 44, 149
Okishio castle 142
Okuda Tadatsugu 82–83
Okuzōin 81
Omasa 9, 11–12, 63, 64

Osaka castle 16, 24–25, 38–42, 44, 46, 48, 52–53, 55, 57, 81, 85–86, 91–92, 125, 162
Osaka o-jin no otomo 38, 42–43, 50, 91
Osaka o-jin o-ninzu tsukeoboe 38, 43–44, 50
Ōshō 147
Otome pond 88

R

Reigan Cave 98–101, 157, 161
Rendai temple 73, 108
Rikan castle 12–14, 21, 67

S

Saiki castle 69
Sakakibara Motonao 45
Sakazaki Naizen 47, 161
Sakurai Yoshikatsu 123
Sanada Yukimura 84, 85
Sasaki Kojirō 10, 23, 60–61, 70, 78–80, 98, 101, 105, 113–20, 142, 157, 159–60
Sawamura Daigakunosuke Yoshishige 145
Sawayama castle 2
Sekkai shrine 5, 68
Sengoku Hidehisa 16
Senhime 17, 25
Shinmen Higo 9
Shinmen kaki 7, 9
Shinmen Munesada 8–12, 68
Shinmen Munetsura 8–9, 63, 150
Shinmen Muni 7–14, 27–29, 38, 51, 64, 65, 6–71, 107–108, 130, 141, 150

Shinran 76
Shintō Musō-*ryū* 123
Shiota Hamanosuke 136–37,
    139, 142, 144–45, 149
Shisen monastery 75, 77
Shitennō temple 85
Shōden Katori Shintō-*ryū* 123
Shoji Jineimon 26
Shoji Kasutomi 26
Shōrenan temple 2, 6, 69
Shōtoku Taishi 5
Sōda Hōsei 90
Sōkyū sama o-degatari 46, 57
Susuki Kanesuke 83
Suya no Saka 71

T

Taiheiki 9, 72
Taishō temple 19, 103–104,
    142, 146–48, 157, 163
Takada Masayuki 155–56
Takada Matabei Yoshitsugu 119,
    131
Takagi Umanosuke Shigesada
    94, 133
Takeda Shingen 1, 27–28, 64,
    149
Takeyama castle 8, 11, 63
Takuan Sōhō 147
Tanji Hōkin 15, 26, 29, 33, 38,
    51, 69, 73, 95, 130, 151
Tanukidani Fūdō monastery
    71–72
Tasumi Masahisa 14, 17, 67
Tawara Hisamitsu 14, 20
Terao Magonojō Nobumasa
    149, 151, 153
Terao Magoshirō 149

Terao Motomenosuke Nobuyuki
    103, 153
Terao Nobuyuki 103, 149, 151,
    152–53
Terao Sakuzaemon 151
Toda Seigen 113, 120
Toda Shigemasa 114
Toda Yosaemon 80
Toda-*ryū* 87, 113, 120
Tōgun-*ryū* 87
Tokugawa Hidetada 17, 55, 77,
    92, 134
Tokugawa Ieyasu 16, 59, 69–70,
    77, 92, 125–26, 128, 133
Tokugawa Tsugutomo 40
Tokugawa Yorinobu 133
Tokugawa Yoshinao 89, 92, 125
Tomari jinja munefuda 3, 19
Tomari shrine 16, 19, 35
Tomida castle 8, 12
Tomiku castle 37, 48, 52, 69,
    97, 115, 159
Toneri Shinnō 68
Tōri-*ryū* 10
Torii Mototada 49, 50
Tōsakushi 1, 3, 7, 9, 11, 24, 28,
    30, 63, 65, 66, 68, 157–58
Toyoda Masanaga 61, 97
Toyotomi Hideyori 61, 81, 162
Toyotomi Hideyoshi 8, 13, 20,
    143, 145
Tsunomure castle 69

U

U no mane 132
Ukita Hideie 2, 8–9, 12, 150
Ukita Naoie 8, 12, 149
Usuki castle 69

W

Watanabe Kōan 34

Y

Yagyū Munenori 78, 92, 125–26, 147

Yagyū Shinkage-*ryū* 92, 125–26, 137, 139, 160

Yagyū Toshiyoshi 92, 125

Yashirō Mitsunari 139, 160

Yatsushiro castle 139

Yoshikawa Eiji 10, 39, 42, 65, 127

Yoshiko 2, 6, 12–14, 17, 21, 66–67

Yoshioka Denshichirō Naoshige 108, 111

Yoshioka Kenpō 108

Yoshioka Matashichirō 76, 108, 111–12

Yoshioka Naokata 107

Yoshioka Naomitsu 107

Yoshioka Naomoto 106–107

Yoshioka Seijūrō Naotsuna 108–110

Yoshioka-*ryū* 106–108

 TOYO Press publishes books that contribute to a deeper understanding of Asian cultures. Editorial supervision: William de Lange. Book and cover design: Chōkei Studios. Printing and binding: IngramSpark. The typeface used is Gill Sans.

www.ingramcontent.com/pod-product-compliance
Lightning Source LLC
LaVergne TN
LVHW020607200726
843509LV00001B/7